Praise for
Enjoy

"In *Enjoy*, Trillia Newbell draws us toward a better understanding of the goodness of God. She invites us to give ourselves permission not just to see his goodness, but to savor it in tangible ways in the simple pleasures of life. Her message is challenging and freeing, practical and personal, spoken with the graciousness that characterizes her life and ministry. I was drawn to reflect on my tendency to misuse or take for granted God's good gifts, and I was reminded that enjoying them as they were intended to be enjoyed is nothing less than an act of worship."

—JEN WILKIN, Bible teacher and author of *Women of the Word*

"I can't think of anyone who better epitomizes the theme of this book than Trillia Newbell! Her joyful spirit and big-as-the-world smile are infectious and emanate from a woman who, in the midst of a broken world, has found true, robust joy in our God who is making all things new and has given us countless good gifts to enjoy."

—NANCY DEMOSS WOLGEMUTH, author, host/teacher of *Revive Our Hearts*

"Trillia Newbell writes with wisdom and grace on why Christians can and should take joy in the gifts that God has given us. This practical book will help all Christians see how the gospel transforms every part of our lives. Trillia Newbell is a gift to the church."

—RUSSELL MOORE, president, Southern Baptist Ethics & Religious Liberty Commission

"Are you weary of contrived checklists and lackluster limitations that stifle faith and steal your joy? This book is the breath of fresh air you've been craving. In this delightfully refreshing read, Trillia invites us, indeed, to taste and see that the Lord is good—and so is this glorious world and everything in it. God has given us all good things to enjoy, and this book sets us free to relish every moment of every aspect of our lives."

—DEIDRA RIGGS, author of *Every Little Thing*

"In her new book *Enjoy,* Trillia Newbell warmly invites us to the forgotten feast of joyful living. She reveals how we can find delight in our duties, pleasure in our play, fellowship in our friendships, and wonder in our world. Most of all, she faithfully encourages our enjoyment of God as we enjoy the gifts he's given."

—MELISSA KRUGER, author of *The Envy of Eve* and
Walking with God in the Season of Motherhood

"I grew up in the church. I've heard literally thousands of messages canvassing almost every topic you can imagine. Almost. I have never in my life heard a single message that God has green-lighted me to simply enjoy him and all of the gifts he has for me—until now. My friend Trillia Newbell has done both Christians and those curious about Christ a great service. She's eulogized the 'curmudgeon God,' portrayed by so many Christians throughout the centuries and has unleashed a smiling God who wants his children to come alive through the gifts he's given us. I so wish I had read this decades ago."

—BRYAN LORITTS, lead pastor of Abundant Life Christian
Fellowship and author of *Saving the Saved*

"As you walk with Christ and mature, you come to realize true Christians live in a state well described by the apostle Paul: 'Sorrowful, yet always rejoicing.' Trillia Newbell has the ability to point you to real joy in Jesus while not ignoring the pain that's an ever-present reality for us all. You will find real comfort in her biblical exposition of this world's beauty without sugarcoating the bitter parts of Christian life. I truly appreciate an author capable of such balance."

—AIXA LÓPEZ, blogger at Corazón a Papel (*Heart to Paper*); pastor's wife; and board member, Christian Alliance for Orphans (CAFO) of Guatemala

"God is mighty and powerful, all knowing and everywhere at once. These are good truths. God is also a loving Father who gives good gifts to be enjoyed deeply by his children. Christians should belly laugh often, enjoy dinner with friends, and be awestruck by the beauty of God's creation. In *Enjoy,* Trillia does a masterful job of helping us learn to enjoy God's good graces to us."

—MATT CHANDLER, lead pastor, teaching, The Village Church

"Can we honor God by enjoying his good gifts? Boldly and simply, Trillia Newbell says yes. Take up her practical and biblical challenge to find delight in the everyday. Most important, let your heart brim with gratitude and praise for the Giver of all good things."

—JEN POLLOCK MICHEL, award-winning author of *Teach Us to Want* and *Keeping Place*

"Trillia J. Newbell has an infectious joy. Her joy in the Lord and the good gifts he gives us bursts forth from these pages like a firecracker on a summer night, like a flow of water between the rocks, like an uncontainable word of praise for a job well done. This book, like its author, is a delight."

—KAREN SWALLOW PRIOR, PhD, author of *Booked* and *Fierce Convictions* enjoy

enjoy

Finding the Freedom to Delight Daily
in God's Good Gifts

Trillia J. Newbell

MULTNOMAH

Enjoy

All Scripture quotations, unless otherwise indicated, are taken from the ESV® Bible (the Holy Bible, English Standard Version®), copyright © 2001 by Crossway, a publishing ministry of Good News Publishers. Used by permission. All rights reserved. Scripture quotations marked (NASB) are taken from the New American Standard Bible®. Copyright © 1960, 1962, 1963, 1968, 1971, 1972, 1973, 1975, 1977, 1995 by the Lockman Foundation. Used by permission. (www.Lockman.org). Scripture quotations marked (NIV) are taken from the Holy Bible, New International Version®, NIV®. Copyright © 1973, 1978, 1984 by Biblica Inc.™ Used by permission. All rights reserved worldwide.

Trade Paperback ISBN 978-1-60142-852-3
eBook ISBN 978-1-60142-853-0

Copyright © 2016 by Trillia J. Newbell

Cover design by Kristopher K. Orr

Published in the United States by Multnomah, an imprint of the Crown Publishing Group, a division of Penguin Random House LLC, New York.

MULTNOMAH® and its mountain colophon are registered trademarks of Penguin Random House LLC.

Library of Congress Cataloging-in-Publication Data
Names: Newbell, Trillia J., author.
Title: Enjoy : finding the freedom to delight daily in God's good gifts / Trillia J. Newbell.
Description: First Edition. | Colorado Springs, Colorado : Multnomah, 2016. | Includes
    bibliographical references.
Identifiers: LCCN 2016038847 (print) | LCCN 2016040507 (ebook) | ISBN
    9781601428523 (pbk.) | ISBN 9781601428530 (electronic)
Subjects: LCSH: Joy—Religious aspects—Christianity. | Pleasure—Religious
    aspects—Christianity. | Spirituality—Christianity. | Glory of God.
Classification: LCC BV4647.J68 N48 2016 (print) | LCC BV4647.J68 (ebook) | DDC
    248.4—dc23
LC record available at https://lccn.loc.gov/2016038847

Printed in the United States of America
2016—First Edition

10 9 8 7 6 5 4 3 2 1

SPECIAL SALES
Most Multnomah books are available at special quantity discounts when purchased in bulk by corporations, organizations, and special-interest groups. Custom imprinting or excerpting can also be done to fit special needs. For information, please e-mail specialmarketscms@penguinrandomhouse.com or call 1-800-603-7051.

This book is dedicated to my kids,
Weston and Sydney.
Life will get difficult, but God is
truly good and faithful.
Believe in him. Lean on him.
I pray you learn to delight in him
and enjoy his good gifts to you.
May you glorify God and enjoy
him forever.

Contents

1

An Invitation to Enjoy

A few years ago I bought a bike. Not just any old bike, but a Specialized road bike, which is a style often used for racing or longer rides. After spending a couple of months mostly sitting to finish up several writing projects, I wanted a new and interesting outlet for fitness. A good friend is an avid cyclist, and hearing his delight in the sport made me that much more curious. So instead of testing the waters, I just jumped straight in.

Let me tell you, I love cycling. For so many reasons. I'm never more aware of God's beautiful creation than while riding through it on my bike. I'm drawn to worship and rejoice and thank God for his gifts, like oxygen, trees, and the horses I ride past on one of my routes. Not to mention how much I benefit from the exercise, which helps me focus with renewed energy when I return to the tasks of my day.

But here's the thing: simply enjoying my time on the bike didn't feel right to me. It seemed that my cycling needed to have a greater purpose, that the time invested needed to be legitimized by something with deeper meaning. So not long after I bought the road bike, I began training for a triathlon. I connected with an organization I love and built a fundraiser out of my leisure activity. That felt right. The problem is, it wasn't.

As I began to formalize my plans, I connected with a leader of the organization I wanted to fundraise for. Soon I realized that what he desired me to do and what I actually had the time for wasn't possible. I couldn't finish all the projects for the fundraising effort and train and still have time for the rest of my life activities related to work and family. It quickly became too much for me. In the end, a small wreck on my bike put me out of training for a few months. In terms of triathlon training, especially when new to the sport, that's a long time. In the end, I missed my race. I was terribly sad but realized God was teaching me much through this situation.

I started to recognize the importance of knowing my limits and learning the discipline of saying no. But beyond that, I began to ask myself why I felt I couldn't have a hobby solely for the purpose of enjoyment. Why did I wrestle with guilt over time spent riding my bike, feeling as if it were a waste of time unless I turned it into something greater? Could a leisure activity possibly be a way to glorify God?

In the months since, I've discovered the answer is a definite yes.

Have you, too, struggled with whether it's okay to enjoy something in your life, such as maintaining a flower garden or sitting down to read or dancing with your husband? I imagine I'm not alone in feeling confused about the purpose and significance of leisure, as well as other pleasures in life, and I'd love to share with you some of what I've discovered. In this book, you and I will consider together why God gave us things like leisure, relationships, work, creation, and sex. And my prayer is that in learning to better enjoy, recognize, and appreciate these gifts, we'll learn to more clearly see and more passionately worship the provider of all these good gifts.

GOD'S INVITATION TO ENJOY

The world has its share of dark and difficult things. After all, life is not all rainbows and butterflies. I know this all too well, having experienced the deaths of dear loved ones, the pain of unfair criticism, and the agony of miscarriages. Yet the Bible specifically instructs us to rejoice in our sorrows, to delight and give thanks. Does this mean we're supposed to walk around pretending everything is okay? I don't think so.

The apostle Paul, writing to the church in Corinth, unpacked this apparent paradox. After describing the various sufferings he and his companions had endured, Paul wrote of being "sorrowful, yet always rejoicing" (2 Corinthians 6:10). He didn't pretend life was easy. He acknowledged the hardships he had endured, and yet he also recognized that he had a great Savior and, as a result, much reason for rejoicing.

Paul continued this theme in 1 Thessalonians: "Rejoice always, pray without ceasing, give thanks in all circumstances; for this is the will of God in Christ Jesus for you" (5:16–18). He also revealed that joy is a fruit of the Spirit—something that is developed and nurtured within us by his presence in our lives and by his grace (see Galatians 5:22). So we can conclude that we *need* God in order to have true and lasting joy.

The reality is that you and I live in a fallen world, yet at the same time, God has given us abundantly more than we could ask for or imagine. You and I have been given gifts upon gifts from God, gifts he intends for our enjoyment. In the pages to come, we are going to think on these things and even experiment with how we can move beyond recognition of these wonderful gifts to practical delight in them.

So what does it look like to truly enjoy? I think God lays it out for us in 1 Thessalonians, in the verse we just looked at. Our enjoyment is all about him. He gives good gifts, and we in turn thank him. But we not only thank God—we experience the fullness of enjoyment as we let those gifts point us to truths about him.

Think about your favorite dish. My mouth begins to water as I imagine taking a bite of a strawberry dipped in Nutella. Eating a strawberry can seem so trivial until we begin to reflect on the Giver of the gift. Knowing who is behind the gift brings significance to that food and prompts an attitude of thanksgiving. We can enjoy every single bite to the glory of God (see 1 Corinthians 10:31).

The reality, however, is that nothing in this world can be truly fulfilling. The whole earth groans for the new heaven and earth (see Romans 8:22). We long for something better. It's a longing that won't be fulfilled here—not now, not on this earth. The president of Desiring God ministries, Jon Bloom, summed up this sentiment well:

> Right now even the best things are not what they should
> be. And so much goes so very wrong. In this partial age,
> our bodies, our loved ones, our careers, our creations, our
> investments, and our plans are all subject to the forces of
> futility (Romans 8:20). This age is marked more by

suffering (8:18), longing (8:19), groaning (8:23), and hope (8:24) than by fulfillment.[1]

I think the Preacher in Ecclesiastes would have given Bloom a hearty "Amen!" When I read the first few sentences of Ecclesiastes, it makes me want to throw in the towel and head straight to heaven! "All is vanity," he proclaims. Why bother with toil, or anything else for that matter? Yet if you keep reading, you see redemption. You see why we participate in the everyday activities of life: it's all vanity, sure, but it's all a gift from our heavenly Father! Consider these biblical contrasts:

Toil is exhausting (2:22–23); rejoice in God's good gift of work (5:19).

The toil to eat and drink is vain (Psalm 127:2); eating, drinking, and work are God's gift to man (Ecclesiastes 3:12–13).

There's much to lament about, but we can and should enjoy, delight, and rejoice. Zack Eswine, pastor of Riverside Church in St. Louis, Missouri, puts it like this: "[The Preacher in Ecclesiastes] maintains that God exists and is knowable. Therefore purpose can be recovered, not beneath the sun, but in the One who created the sun."[2]

Purpose. There must be purpose in order for us to make sense of the world. That purpose isn't found in the world; it's found only in God. If, as *The Westminster Catechism* declares, the chief end (or purpose) of man is "to glorify God, and to enjoy him forever,"[3] then part of enjoying God now is learning to enjoy what he has done, what he has given, and what he has created.

Let's start our adventure into more fully enjoying God by looking at one of the first things he revealed about himself in the Bible.

GOD DELIGHTS

In Genesis 1 God created the heavens and the earth, and what did he say? Not "I did an okay job." No, he delighted in all he created. He said it was good and then *very* good! This wasn't a half-hearted proclamation. He announced "It is good" with the same power as when he said, "Let there be light."

Notice also as you read through the creation story that each time God created something, he paused and said it was good.[4] He didn't wait until the end of all his work and then declare it good. All along the way, every detail was thoughtfully created—and it was good. The light, sea, animals, and plants—he saw that they were all good.

I'm not especially creative when it comes to art, but I do love to cook. As I think about God creating the whole earth, it reminds me of what it's like to cook a meal, though this example certainly will fall short! When I roast fresh vegetables, for example, I need to gather the ingredients—sweet potatoes, red onions, Yukon potatoes, carrots, turnips, leeks, garlic, and maybe a little cauliflower—and then slice and dice. It's not uncommon for me to pause and take a picture of the raw vegetables because, to me, there's unique beauty and goodness in the sliced vegetables. I usually delight in the aroma of one of the spices I decide to toss in along with the olive oil. Even now, writing this, I had to take a brief moment to close my eyes and imagine the smell! After forty minutes of roasting in the oven and occasional tossing to mix the flavors, I pull the vegetables out. Again, I'm reminded that it's good. And that's only the sight and fragrance! When I taste the explosion of flavors, the goodness of these foods is evident to me.

Now, let's go back to Genesis 1. Can you imagine the delight God must have experienced when he created all things and they were perfect? I get such joy out of cooking a panful of vegetables—surely when God said his creation was good, he meant it in the purest, most delightful way. What he made was very good. That our holy, awesome God would take pleasure in his creation and declare its goodness is truly amazing.

When I think about the creation story, it's not hard for me to imagine how the Lord could make the sea and say it's good, or plants and animals and say they are good. But think about how the Lord knew that one day man would sin against him and that this sin would affect every aspect of his beautiful creation, yet he still created us and said man was good. It is unbelievably remarkable to me. The author of Psalm 8 captures my thoughts well:

> When I look at your heavens, the work of your
>   fingers,
>   the moon and the stars, which you have set in
>   place,
> what is man that you are mindful of him,
>   and the son of man that you care for him?
>
> Yet you have made him a little lower than the heav-
>   enly beings
>   and crowned him with glory and honor.
> You have given him dominion over the works of your
>   hands;
>   you have put all things under his feet,
> all sheep and oxen,

and also the beasts of the field,
the birds of the heavens, and the fish of the sea,
whatever passes along the paths of the seas.

O Lord, our Lord,
how majestic is your name in all the earth!
(verses 3–9)

I look to Genesis 1, and I see God's amazing handiwork and marvel that he delights in man. Zephaniah 3:17 tells us that God rejoices over us. This is true even after the Fall. What amazing grace! And we know that God so loved the world that he gave his Son for us. It's astonishing and humbling. It shouldn't be this way, but it is.

So how does all this relate to our delight in God's gifts? What's the opportunity for you and me?

As God's image bearers, you and I have the capacity to reflect certain aspects of our heavenly Father. And there is no doubt he has given us the same capacity to declare over his creation that it is good. We can rejoice and delight and find joy in what he has given us. But as sons and daughters of Adam and Eve, we must also contend with those things that tempt us not to enjoy.

DISTORTED BY THE FALL

Of all creation, we know that man was unique. Adam and Eve were created in the image of God and given dominion over everything else. After creating mankind, God finished his work and declared that it was very good. And then he rested. (So *rest* must be a good thing, right?)

So here we are. God has created Eden and placed earth's first people in the garden to work it. Work was part of his original design, even in paradise! God gave them everything they would need—I imagine it was actually *far* beyond what they could ever need. There was only one rule: don't eat from the tree of the knowledge of good and evil. From our vantage point, it doesn't seem like a tough request. *Hey—you've got all you need. Surely you can abstain from eating from this one tree, right?* But we know how this ended, and it wasn't pretty. Eve fell into Satan's trap, the couple ate the apple, their eyes were opened to good and evil, they tried to clothe themselves, and finally they hid from God. The world was forever changed as a result of their disobedience. What was once beautiful had now been marred by sin.

It would be easy for me to self-righteously declare that, in their place, I wouldn't have eaten that fruit. I'd like to think I would have self-control, that I wouldn't covet, that I wouldn't fall for the lies of the devil and question God's goodness for me and commands for living. God had given them so much to enjoy, yet they decided it wasn't enough. The truth is that the same lies we see in Genesis 3 often hinder us today from enjoying what God has given to us.

As I noted earlier, true and right enjoyment focuses on God, on delighting and enjoying him forever. But because of the Fall, our approach toward enjoyment seems to fall into two different categories: either you and I are fully engaged in hedonistically pursuing our joy and fulfillment in the things of this earth, or we fear that anything we take joy in is ultimately sinful and selfish. We live either as if the world were our playground and everything is ultimately about us and our fulfillment or as if we were wasting precious time if not engaged in serious pursuits.

Some may suggest the solution is simply to live a little and enjoy what God has made as long as you're careful to thank him as you delight. As I've thought and studied, I don't think this is how one truly enjoys. It's not that we find something we enjoy and then try to cram God into it. We enjoy because we know that the gift is given by God for our enjoyment. The gift starts with God as the Giver. If we believe this and see all things as his gifts to us, we are free to abandon our man-made rules and self-imposed guilt and simply enjoy.

Discontentment

But fixing our eyes on the Giver is rarely our natural response to good gifts. Sometimes it can be a struggle even to recognize certain things in our lives as gifts.

My children are incredibly grateful kids, but every now and then I'll see this struggle played out in their response to something I've given them. You probably know what I'm talking about. You've labored in the kitchen for hours, or maybe just five minutes, but at least you're making an effort to feed them, right? You set a plateful of love in the shape of food in front of one of your kids only to hear, "I don't want that." *What? You don't want it? Do you want to eat at all?* We may be tempted to pull out the classic line, "There are kids who have nothing, so you'd better eat this."

The truth is, we can be just like our kids. We can have so much and then say to God, "I don't want that."

My husband and I attend a church small group that includes a great mix of personalities. Not one of us is similar, actually. Recently, this was highlighted during our prayer time. Winter was on the horizon, and I confessed to the group that I tend to become melancholy and despondent in the winter, when it's dark, cold, and rainy. I know this is influenced by the seasons, because the moment the sun comes out in the spring, my demeanor changes—I'm lighter and feel a sense of joy as I see life return to the earth. So this year I thought I'd take action and ask for prayer. Another woman in my group is the exact opposite. She loves winter and rain—lots of rain. I would pray for sunshine, and she would pray for downpours! Besides having a good laugh and fighting over prayer requests during those winter days, I realized the Lord was showing me something about enjoyment: when my heart is discontented, it's hard for me to see God's work and gifts.*

I've prayed for some time now that the Lord would help me enjoy the darkness of winter. He answered the prayer—not by taking away the dark but by helping me think of creative ways to enjoy it.

One memorable Saturday, the temperatures were low and a chilly rain was pouring. I set up our little music system, pulled out some games, and opened a sliding glass door to the back porch so we could hear the rain, and our family began to play and sing together. It was one of the most delightful Saturday mornings we've had. The darkness remained and the rain still fell, but by focusing not on my discontentment but on the gift of a slow day at home with my family, I found a reason to enjoy the rain. I'm not saying every rainy day is like that, but it did serve as a reminder to me that God is good even in the darkness.

A lack of contentment isn't the only reason we might struggle with enjoyment, but it is likely one of the root causes. We may desire a different home, child, husband, job, body, meal, or even

---

* Seasonal Affective Disorder (SAD) is a real disease that affects many. For more information, resources, or help, visit the Christian Counseling and Education Foundation at www.ccef.org.

lifestyle for various reasons, but at the root you'll likely find a heart wrestling with contentment. Perhaps you've had the thought, *If I only had* _____, *then I would be joyful*, or *If he'd only change that aspect of his personality, then our marriage would be perfect and I could enjoy him.*

I would go so far as to say that if we can learn to be content, we can know the joys of life in any circumstance and declare along with Paul the famous words of Philippians 4: "For I have learned in whatever situation I am to be content" (verse 11). Paul was persecuted, imprisoned, and abandoned by his friends, and yet he learned to be content. Jeremiah Burroughs, a seventeenth-century Puritan writer, made this observation about this passage: "The doctrinal conclusion briefly is this: That to be well skilled in the mystery of Christian contentment is the duty, glory, and excellence of a Christian."[5] That's a fairly strong statement, don't you think? But I'm convinced that, by the grace of God, we too can train ourselves to be content in any and every circumstance.

Paul learned to be content, and it resulted in peace. But what if he had instead grown angry, resentful, and cynical because of his circumstances? I imagine we might have different epistles! But beyond that, his personal life and well-being would have been strained. He would have, of course, remained in relationship with God because of Jesus, but that relationship would also have been strained. If Paul had not fought for contentment, perhaps he would have given up on ministry or would have begun serving the Lord in resentment rather than out of love. If Paul hadn't fought for contentment and joy during his suffering, he may have assumed that God left him to suffer alone. But Paul understood the eternal glory and reward that was awaiting him. When we don't receive what we think we deserve and allow discontentment to consume us, the result is grumbling, complaining, frustration, and anger. We begin to view the world and everyone in it, including God, as being set against us. In our discontentment, we often stiff-arm the Lord's good gifts to us, and instead of receiving and enjoying, we grumble. We see fault in them, or we long for something else. It's as if he brought his bride, the church, to a feast with Gulf Coast shrimp and we asked for a Big Mac instead.

What God chooses to give us is infinitely better than what we think we want or need. This, among other reasons, is why we want to fight to be content with what the Lord gives us.

Ingratitude

Part of this battle to receive good gifts from God is reflected in the way we receive good gifts from other people. I wonder if Paul recognized this as he described his interaction with the Philippian church. As we read on to verses 14–20, we get a glimpse of the remarkable relationship between the Philippian church and Paul. The church continually showered Paul with gifts, as if they couldn't help themselves. They wanted Paul to know how grateful they were for his labors on their behalf. And Paul never once sought the gifts! He received them only because he knew it would bring the Christians joy and also because he knew their sacrifice was a fragrant offering to the Lord. He realized the value of their giving went well beyond simply supplying his needs.

This relationship serves as an example for our own earthly relationships. I definitely have friends and family whom I love dearly, and I can't help but shower them with gifts. But what if Paul had continually refused their gifts? What if my friends and family did the same? What if he mocked them or sent their gifts back? What if Paul never thanked them? Surely we give without the need for thanks, but the gratitude of the receiver is a kind blessing. I'd be sad, maybe even slightly hurt, and definitely confused if my gifts met with resistance, especially from those I love most. Why wouldn't someone want something that is good?

What Paul probably realized was that the kindness and love of the Philippian church toward him was an extension of God's care and love for him. After thanking them for their gifts and stating that he was well supplied because of their generosity, he pointed their attention (and his!) back to the Lord: "And my God will supply every need of yours according to his riches in glory in Christ Jesus" (verse 19).

Sometimes our pride keeps us from receiving and being thankful for good things from others. We don't like to receive. Our pride keeps us from wanting to appear needy. We can fear that receiving good gifts from others might reveal our need or even our inadequacy. But in our relationship with the Lord, we offer nothing; all we *can* do is receive. Sure, we can offer praise and we can thank him, but again, it's all because of him. It's all about him.

When we understand that everything we have and do in this life is from and about him, you and I can guard against the temptation to worship the creature and the created rather than the Creator. In other words, we can enjoy life while also remembering to give God the glory for what we have or do or taste or see. We receive graciously with thanksgiving, rather than pursuing gifts for their own sake, which can lead to sexual immorality, impurity, idolatry, jealously, rivalries, envy, and other "works of the flesh" (Galatians 5:19–21). As we find our joy in the Lord, our hearts become content and we find our lives characterized by fruit of the Spirit, such as love, joy, peace, patience, kindness, faithfulness, and self-control.

Guilt

Because of the Fall we sometimes fail to recognize the "good" of God's gifts and, like Adam and Eve, reach for something we think we'll like more. Other times we fail to recognize the Giver of those gifts, and again we focus on feeding our desires. Yet another effect of the Fall is that we're tempted to ignore the various gifts God has given us because of guilt. We struggle with feeling as if were wrong to enjoy them. Maybe you think, *I shouldn't eat that. I shouldn't care about how my home is decorated. Sitting on a beach is a waste of time.* Remember my bike? Yeah, guilt is exactly what I was experiencing.

But hasn't God given us dominion over all creation? One of the first things God did when he created male and female was to declare that they had dominion over the earth. God told them, "Be fruitful and multiply and fill the earth and subdue it, and have dominion over . . . every living thing that moves on the earth" (Genesis 1:28).

Please don't misunderstand me; I'm not calling for a reckless rule without thought or concern over how to wield our dominion. God has given us a great responsibility and honor, and we must steward his world to the best of our ability. How that looks for you and for me may vary, but the command to glorify him in it remains universal. To eat, drink, and do all things to the glory of God means not abusing the good things he has given to us. But I think we forget that we have dominion over the earth. Instead of enjoying it, we lament, worry, and feel guilt when we attempt to delight in the things the Lord has given us. Again, the gift giving started with God in Genesis 1, and you and I need to remember that the gifts we experience today begin with God too.

As I reflect on the Fall of man, it's humbling to see how

similar we are to Eve. Her sin isn't all that different from our sin and struggles today. But our difficulties in fully enjoying God's gifts to us aren't just related to Eve's temptation. As I mentioned earlier, we often find it difficult to simply enjoy the things of earth. We believe we must have a great purpose in our pursuit of them. Our hobbies must be legitimized or incentivized. Or maybe shame leads us to believe we don't deserve to enjoy anything. In view of the people suffering around the world, and sometimes in our own lives, how can we sit here and enjoy our relationships, sex, food, arts, creation, and more?

NOT THE END OF THE STORY

It would be tragic if the story ended with a world broken by Adam and Eve's sin. Thankfully, it doesn't. God always had a plan of redemption for the world. He sent his Son to redeem the world, and that alone is means for great rejoicing. And in time, all things will be made new.

But well before Matthew 1, God cared immediately for the needs of Adam and Eve. He sent them out of the garden clothed with garments of skins. God cares deeply for his creatures and is indeed the Giver of good gifts. In the meantime, we can live in the certainty that although our world is absolutely fallen and stained by sin, God's gifts are all around us.

The Fall of man introduced sin and decay into God's perfect setting. But God is a God who redeems. Not only does he delight and rejoice in his creation, but he's also given you and me the capability to enjoy, delight in, and give thanks for all he has created.

But how can we live this reality on a daily basis?

The Enjoy Project

My goal for this book is that, together, you and I will gain a deeper understanding of what it means to delight daily in God's good gifts—and that we'll put that understanding into practice. So I designed The Enjoy Project as a tool to help us put our faith into action.

Please bear in mind that the project is *not* a must-do list. In other words, you can enjoy God's gifts without completing any of these steps. And you certainly aren't obligated to do this in order to please God. This is simply a list of suggestions to help us all— that's it! So if attempting the project will add to your stress or not completing it will leave you feeling as if you've failed, please don't attempt the project. It's simply here for you to use as much or as little as is helpful for you. Now that you understand what The Enjoy Project is *not,* let me explain what it *is.*

When I told you about my cycling experience, I mentioned that I jumped straight into the sport and took off. That's true—kind of. I bought the bike, but not until after some thorough research and asking advice from my cycling friends. I then bought a book about triathlon training and joined a triathlon team to get a little help. I knew I wanted to do it, and although I had the necessary tool (the bike), I realized it would be helpful to have a little push—teammates and trusted friends to cheer me on and guide me. My hope is that this book will be a tool and The Enjoy Project will help propel and guide you and me along the way to enjoyment.

At the end of each chapter, we'll pause to consider seven or eight ideas for how we can put to use what we're learning. Assuming you read a chapter per week, the project will give you ideas for applying that week's insights while reading the next chapter. The goal is to put into practice at least one item per chapter, or as many as you are able to, with the hope that you'll eventually do all seven. Of course, feel free to do whatever you'd prefer. If you would like to try one a day, hitting all seven in the week, go for it!

The point of the project is simply to begin to put into action what you've learned, in ways that will increase your own enjoyment—and often enrich the lives of others.

I'd like to encourage you to keep a journal for each week. Again, this is not a rule, simply a suggested way to track what you experience during the Project as your eyes are opened to new opportunities to delight in God's goodness. I don't think you need to write pages and pages, but a paragraph detailing your daily experience might prove useful.

God encourages us to recount his goodness, so perhaps journaling your Enjoy Project will help you remember God's faithfulness and take note of how you and others were affected by it.

The Enjoy Project is developed in such a way that it could be done completely on your own, but if you can, grab a friend (or two or three) to do it with you. If you decide to do it in a group, schedule a consistent time to connect and exchange notes, share fun stories, and encourage one other. Help your friend resist the temptation to feel guilty while she's trying to enjoy!

In summary, here's what it looks like:

1. Find The Enjoy Project at the end of each chapter.

2. Decide which suggestion(s) you'd like to try.

3. Schedule a day to do it, and map out a plan, if needed.

4. Do it.

5. Journal about the experience. How effective was it? Were you able to enjoy the process? What encouraged you about it? What new thing might you begin enjoying as a result? How did it affect others around you? How was God glorified, or how did you recognize God's goodness through this action?

6. If you're in a group, share your thoughts.

To put the Project to the test, a friend and I decided to do it from start to finish. We were able to take what we were discovering about God, roll up our sleeves, and figure out how to enjoy him and all he has done. I was challenged, encouraged, and inspired. I was amazed to realize what I had been taking for granted. The Project brought intentionality to all that we were doing and thinking about. It truly was a joy!

Before we move on to the Project, just one more word of explanation: You'll notice that the seventh suggestion for each week is to "pray and preach the gospel to yourself." I've come to realize that, as followers of Christ, we are what I call leaky vessels. We forget to remember that it is the gospel—the reality that Jesus died on the cross, bearing the wrath that we deserved, and is now seated at the right hand of the Father on our behalf—that enables us to live and enjoy life. The gospel isn't something we simply hear once and move on from; it should guide our every moment. If you have placed your faith and trust in the finished work of the cross, then you are clothed with Christ's righteousness. We can all approach the throne of grace because of Jesus. Of all God's good gifts to us, salvation should be the one we delight in at every opportunity.

The Enjoy Project:
An Invitation to Enjoy

This is the beginning of The Enjoy Project! Here are your suggestions for practicing joy this week:

1. Decide how you will document your journey, whether by journaling, starting a blog series, or some other means. If you are journaling, go ahead and secure a journal.

2. If you've decided that accountability will be a helpful tool, identify who you will invite to join you in The Enjoy Project.

3. There is beautiful fruit that can come from learning to enjoy. What are a few areas, specifically concerning the fruit of the Spirit listed in Galatians 5:22–23, in which you hope to grow during this project and as you read the book?

4. Write down aspects of life that you find difficult to enjoy, such as your spouse, children, leisure, work, church. This could be based on a lack of contentment, fear, or guilt—the reason will be worked out in due time. Be honest and vulnerable. There's nothing to fear, and the goal is to increase your joy, so make your list as long or as short as you like, whatever will help you focus your thoughts on tangible goals in the weeks ahead.

5. Write down your hopes for the Project. For example, "I hope to find new ways to enjoy rest, such as learning to take a Sabbath."
6. Look back over the chapter to identify one idea or truth that really stands out. Find a way to put that into practice this week.
7. Pray and preach the gospel to yourself.

Lord, thank you that you are the Giver, that out of your generosity and love you've filled the world and our lives with gifts. Help me to see them, enjoy them, and praise you as a result. Guard my heart against the enemies of joy: discontentment, ingratitude, and guilt. And thank you for the gift of Jesus, who covers all my sin and shortcomings.

God calls us to both

heavenly

purpose and

earthly pleasure.

—Michael Wittmer

The Gift of One

Another

I had recently become a Christian and was longing for strong relationships, especially in my new church. I wasn't convinced deep friendship would happen for me there, since most of the people seemed to have already established their circles of friendship. The Lord, however, gave me not only a friend but a friend who would become like a sister.

I tease Amy that she didn't really view me as friend at first but as more of a project or an assignment. That wasn't her heart at all, but she was in college ministry and was assigned to reach out to the university community I happened to be a part of. We started meeting together with the assumption that she'd simply be discipling me as a new believer. Years later, we now finish each other's sentences, sit on the phone completely silent while the other cries, and laugh so loud and so long that our stomach muscles ache. We are indeed the best of friends.

This relationship hasn't come without hardship. We've had

conflict over our sixteen or so years of constant contact. We've had seasons when we struggled to relate well and understand where the other person was coming from. But we've always been faithful to our friendship, refusing to give up on it. We've always worked through what needed to be worked through. We love one another deeply, and it is made evident by our commitment over these many years.

RELATIONSHIPS ARE A GIFT

As I noted in the previous chapter, God doesn't do anything half-heartedly. When he created the world, he was intentional and thoughtful about every aspect and detail. In Genesis 2:18 he said, "It is not good that the man should be alone." Enough said, right? It is not good for man to be alone, so he created Eve, a helper. He designed marriage for intimacy and procreation. But God didn't leave relationships there. He created humans with a need to be in community to fully thrive. He created the idea of family associated by marriage and birth as well as the family of God. We'll look more closely at the beautiful gift of the Church in a later chapter, but there's no denying God sees this community as a gift—so important that he sent his Son to die for it. We'll explore many scriptures on this subject, often called the "one anothers," that are meant for the edification of people. God intended that we use our gifts, abilities, and words to encourage and benefit others.

God never intended for us to do life on our own. Even Jesus was born into a family and given a mom and dad and brothers. Jesus had friends, not just followers.

The problem with most of our relationships and the reason they are such a mess is that we mix up who and what we are made for. The ultimate relationship God designed us to enjoy is a relationship with him. But sin separated us from his holy presence, so Jesus cleared the way through his death and resurrection.

Too often, instead of worshiping God and making that relationship our main goal, we worship people and make an idol of their thoughts, attitudes, and feelings toward us. We expect from others that which only God can fulfill. Maybe your moods rise and fall based on your standing with other people. When that happens, this good gift from God is twisted.

People will never give you all that you thirst and hunger for. But ours is a God who redeems, and he desires to make things straight in our relationships. Even though they are difficult and even though we twist them, he desires that we receive this gift and learn how to love the people he has given us.

ONE ANOTHERS

The Bible provides us with a beautiful picture of how God calls us to engage with the people in our lives.

In the book of Galatians, the apostle Paul rebuked believers for divisions over circumcision and for holding the new converts to the old law. He wrote,

> For you were called to freedom, brothers. Only do not use your freedom as an opportunity for the flesh, *but through love serve one another.* For the whole law is fulfilled in one word: *"You shall love your neighbor as yourself."* But if you bite and devour one another, watch out that you are not consumed by one another. (Galatians 5:13–15, emphasis mine)

Paul urged them to avoid the temptation to bite and devour one another by instead counting others as more important than themselves. He wanted them to serve and love one another because, as Jesus affirmed, the entire law is summed up in loving God and loving our neighbor.

How do we see this come to life in our relationships? Paul and other biblical writers provided a set of relationship instructions, often called the "one anothers" because they highlight the love and encouragement we should have for one another. These verses primarily focus not on feelings but on intentional pursuits and acts of love. Here's a short version of what we find in Scripture:

- Love one another (John 13:34).
- Be devoted to one another (Romans 12:10).
- Outdo one another in showing honor (Romans 12:10).
- Live in harmony with one another (Romans 12:16).
- Don't put a stumbling block in the way of others (Romans 14:13).
- Accept one another (Romans 15:7).
- Be patient with one another (Ephesians 4:2).
- Be kind, compassionate, and forgiving of one another (Ephesians 4:32).

I could go on and on. But as you look at that list and evaluate your relationships, are you left feeling a bit defeated? When I began researching for this chapter, I thought I was a pretty amazing friend. I thought I was faithful, forbearing, kind—everything a friend should be. Don't get me wrong; I've had my fair share of broken relationships. But overall I have some dear lifelong friends. Yet each and every one of those friendships, I realized, has experienced some division or conflict at some point. I haven't always been devoted to my friends. I haven't always lived in harmony. I haven't always been patient. In realizing this, my bubble of pride burst. But the Lord has been faithful in each of those relationships to humble me and teach me how to love better. We won't always perfectly live out the one anothers, but we can grow. It's a hard lesson but one I'm thankful for.

Why are relationships so hard? And are they really worth the trouble?

I believe that one of the places we most plainly see the effects of the Fall is in our relationships. As we look at the many divisions and wars between peoples and nations, we see that clearly something has gone awry in the way we relate to and view one another. But we don't really need to look to the wars outside. One glimpse into our heart toward others—think of how you might respond when someone cuts you off in traffic or leaves dirty clothes all over the floor—and we know that something has gone wrong within ourselves as well.

In the beginning Adam and Eve had it all together, something that has never been true since sin entered the world. Their relationship with each other was completely harmonious, pure, lacking in any ill motive or intent. Their love for each other was also pure in the truest sense of the word. They weren't bitter, didn't envy, didn't lust after another, and weren't trying to escape from each other. But as you know, that didn't last long. When God pronounced judgment on the man and woman for looking beyond him for answers to their desires, relationships were forever altered until the day of redemption.

So what did God say as it relates to the Fall's effect on relationships?

To the woman: "I will surely multiply your pain in childbearing; in pain you shall bring forth children. Your desire shall be for your husband, and he shall rule over you" (Genesis 3:16).

To the man: "By the sweat of your face you shall eat bread, till you return to the ground, for out of it you were taken; for you are dust, and to dust you shall return" (Genesis 3:19).

Genesis 3:16 is one of the most researched and debated verses in all of Scripture. What does it mean that the woman would "desire" her husband? Some have interpreted it to mean that she would desire the attention of her husband—that she would idolize his attention. I am sure that part of the Fall involves a desire for men who do not reciprocate that same desire or idolizing the attention of a man, but I believe that the meaning of *desire* here indicates that there will be tension in the marriage. First, God tells Eve that though she has this desire for her husband, "he shall rule over you." That phrase could be an affirmation of the created order, thus highlighting the internal struggle the woman will now feel about her role, or it could mean that he will rule or lead harshly.

However you interpret this passage, we know without a doubt that something in the relationship changed significantly. How sin manifests itself may be different for each person, but all relationships—those of husband and wife, parents and children, coworkers, friends, strangers—have been affected by the Fall and the presence of sin.

One of the ways the Fall has impacted my relationships is in the area of trust. I find it incredibly difficult to trust people. I think people have a tendency to bend truth, to compromise their honesty, or even to outright lie to avoid conflict. (Is this my distrust talking or wisdom? I can't tell.) One of the qualities I value most is honesty. I tend to be extremely honest, maybe to a fault. I think honesty equals integrity, and if you're willing to be dishonest in one area, it's hard for me to trust you'd be honest in other areas. See, this is me being *honest* about my own struggle. And if I've discovered that you've been less than honest or genuine toward me personally, it's incredibly difficult for me to ever fully trust you again. I struggle greatly in this area.

The biblical writer James understood our problems with relationships. I think he would sit me down and say, "Dear Trillia, your passions are at war within you. You desire and do not have, so you murder. (In your heart, dear child, but it's still murder.) You covet and cannot obtain, so what do you do? You fight and quarrel" (see James 4:1–2). James was kind of tough, so I imagine it would be a bit more like a firm rebuke than a pat on the back, but nonetheless, that's what he would tell me. My problem and your problem is that our passions wage war inside us and pour out onto our neighbors.

I'm reminded of the dreadfully sad impact of sin in the story of Cain and Abel. These sons of Adam and Eve seem to have had a tumultuous relationship. At one point, they both brought offerings to the Lord, and the Lord received Abel's but not Cain's. Cain became angry and eventually sought revenge. He killed his brother. I can't imagine the pain this must have caused Adam and Eve.

God provides a warning in the narrative that we'd be wise to heed in regard to relationships. After asking Cain why he was so angry, the Lord warned him (and us!), "And if you do not do well, sin is crouching at the door. Its desire is for you, but you must rule over it" (Genesis 4:7).

In this warning there breathes great hope for you and me. Sin is crouching at the door, *but* you must rule over it. You know what that means? You *can* fight this sin and temptation. Though in this life we'll always battle against sin, you don't have to give in. You don't have to follow through on your anger toward your roommate. You don't have to disregard someone who is different from you. You don't have to slander your neighbor. Now, we most definitely cry out like Paul, "When I want to do right, evil lies close at hand" (Romans 7:21), but we also know that God has given us a spirit of power and love and self-control and we can resist temptation by his Spirit (see 2 Timothy 1:7, 14). This should bring you and me great joy! We will be tempted to sin against others, but at that moment of prompting by the Holy Spirit, we do have a way of escape (see 1 Corinthians 10:13).

Cain didn't take this escape, and he didn't heed God's warning, and as a result, he was punished for his actions.[1] We too will reap the consequences of our actions in our relationships.

I am aware of broken relationships all around me: long friendships that have dissolved over misunderstandings, prodigal sons and daughters, entire congregations that have split, men and women who have left their ministry over disagreements. The list of strained or completely destroyed relationships runs long.

So often the troubles in our relationships are more similar to my story than to Cain and Abel's. We don't physically murder someone. Instead, you may judge a coworker harshly and so instead of enjoying her company, you grumble under your breath or dart the other way when you see her coming. Maybe it's your children. You love them but have zero patience for their disobedience, complaining, whining, or high-energy antics, so you escape them by working extra hours, staring at your phone or computer, or even signing them up for constant activities to get them out of the house. Perhaps you and your spouse seem to be fulfilling the curse in Genesis 3 and your quarrels are never ending. What about that woman who seems to always have it together? You hate her in your heart because of envy and comparison. Or maybe you've been wounded by a parent, sibling, or friend. The examples of how our relationships have been damaged because of sin are endless. Even Jesus experienced the effects of the Fall in his relationships: his friends hurt him—Peter denied him; Judas betrayed him—and yet Jesus went to the cross and died for them, just as he did for us in the midst of our sin.

What about you? Have you experienced relationships distorted by sin? Is there anyone you might need to be reconciled to?

If so, because of Jesus there's hope. By his grace you can put off the sin that clings to you and keeps you from truly enjoying and ultimately loving your neighbors as yourself. If you find yourself in a relationship that needs mending and tender care, know that God has provided a way of escape from our bitterness, anger, resentment, pride, and hate. Through Jesus we can say no to sin and run toward the cross, extending grace to others along the way. As we do this, there is such freedom to enjoy those around us. Our relationships won't be perfect, but I do believe they can be increasingly enjoyable.

THE STING OF DEATH

While pressing into our relationships can be incredibly hard, anticipating the inevitable good-byes can place an additional major strain on us. But in Genesis 3 we see this is another result of the Fall. God said to Adam, "By the sweat of your face you shall eat bread, till you return to the ground, for out of it you were taken; for you are dust, and to dust you shall return" (verse 19).

There's much that's significant about this text, but I want to concentrate on the sting of death. Before the Fall, Adam and Eve would not die and rot. There was no returning to the dirt. Sickness wasn't a problem. Life would go on forever. In the beginning, God created the world and he created it good. God's work is perfect, and he is without iniquity (see Deuteronomy 32:4).

But due to the Fall of man, what was once perfect became accursed, meaning that all things would now die and experience the curse of sin. The judgment of Adam and Eve's one trespass brought condemnation for all (see Romans 5:16).

I was reminded of this painful effect one Wednesday morning when I packed up the kids and headed to my mom's home to pick up my niece. She is a sweet young lady who was in her preteen years at the time. When we met up, I asked my niece how she was doing. She said, "I'm tired of people telling me it's going to be okay. I just want to know what's going to happen next."

A day earlier her mother, my sister, died from what we believe was congestive heart failure. She was only forty years old. Her death came as a shock. At 7:30 p.m. we got a call that she wasn't feeling well, and by 12:30 a.m. she was gone.

My sweet niece is right. To say it's going to be okay isn't all that helpful. I know that the mourning will one day be less heavy. I know that by Monday everyone will once again be busy with life's mundane activities. I also know that one day everything will seem okay. But death is not okay. Death is never okay.

Death is not okay because death is a result of a fallen world. Death is not the way it was meant to be.

Death causes us pain—we mourn, cry, and sometimes get

angry. We also rejoice when we know that our friend or loved one is with Jesus. But even in our rejoicing there's mourning. Death, caused by the Fall, is hard on relationships. We can fear the loss of a loved one and even hesitate to give our hearts fully to another in this fear. It's also incredibly hard to let go of their physical presence, and so we feel an ache for what we once enjoyed. Death is hard on relationships because it's the reality of the end of *all* relationships on this earth.

But—praise God!—there's hope! There's hope because of Jesus. And there's hope because death doesn't hold the final word for us.

In infinite wisdom and grace, God provided a way to conquer death through the work of his Son. Jesus died and rose again in victory. The gift of salvation, through faith in Christ, brings justification, which means we are counted righteous before God, just as if we'd never sinned, just as if we'd always obeyed (see Romans 5:16–17). And this gift is available, absolutely free, to anyone who places their faith in the finished work of the Cross.

God grounds our hope not only in Christ's death but also in his return. On that day death will be swallowed up for good (see 1 Corinthians 15:54). God promises to create a new heaven and new earth, where there'll no longer be "an infant who lives but a few days, or an old man who does not fill out his days" (Isaiah 65:17–25). As the apostle Paul declared, "The last enemy to be destroyed is death" (1 Corinthians 15:26).

When I stare death in the face, I can have hope and faith, not because everything will return to "life as normal," but because a day is coming when I'll never have to face death again. Right now we wait, but one day it will be defeated. It will be defeated for me. It will be defeated for you.

When "the perishable puts on the imperishable, and the mortal puts on immortality," then the words of 1 Corinthians 15:54–57 will finally come true:

Death is swallowed up in victory.
O death, where is your victory?
    O death, where is your sting?

The sting of death is sin, and the power of sin is the law. But thanks be to God, who gives us the victory through our Lord Jesus Christ.

THE CALL TO RADICAL LOVE

Now that we've looked at how the effects of the Fall often hinder our relationships, we are better positioned to truly enjoy them. If our hearts are burdened by self-righteousness, pride, arrogance, or fear, we can remind ourselves of all those one anothers and the great command to love.

Once after I gave a talk in a small town in west Tennessee, a man came up to me to share his thoughts about what it means to be made in the image of God. In short, he shared with me that he could not see how all people are created equal. He believed the Lord made people in different categories with different statuses, which would inevitably mean an inherent God-given class system. I was deeply concerned and saddened by his beliefs. At that moment, I had to make a decision about how to love him while sharing truth. It was incredibly hard—he was a stranger but he was still my neighbor, so to speak. With strangers these sorts of behaviors may leave us confused or even angry for a period, but with those we know and live with, something like this could cause great damage to our relationships. It presents a situation in which you and I might think we could be excused from loving the others involved.

But Jesus calls us to a radical love. These are his words, and they are challenging:

> If you love those who love you, what benefit is that to you? For even sinners love those who love them. And if you do good to those who do good to you, what benefit is that to you? For even sinners do the same. And if you lend to those from whom you expect to receive, what credit is that to you? Even sinners lend to sinners, to get back the same amount. But love your enemies, and do good, and lend, expecting nothing in return, and your reward will be great, and you will be sons of the Most High, for he is kind to the ungrateful and the evil. Be merciful, even as your Father is merciful. (Luke 6:32–36)

These verses were spoken regarding enemies. But knowing that all of the law is summed up in the commandment to love one another and that love is the great commandment, we can safely assume that these verses apply not only to our enemies but also to anyone we need to love. Maybe the coworkers who insist on chatting right outside your office cubicle, the teenager who resents your attempts at guidance, the church member who always has a complaint. Reflect on times of conflict you've had. Could it be you have a skewed view of the person you are struggling with? It can be hard to love someone you view as an enemy or as selfish or as a brat. Your desire and mine should be to love God first and love our neighbors as ourselves. If we can view difficult people as those we are called to love, perhaps it will soften our hearts toward them. This love isn't always reciprocated and isn't always easy. It's tough to love when you don't receive, and yet we must if we are to truly love at all.

What's interesting about relationships is that in order to fully enjoy them, we must be focused on others. The moment we begin to focus on what we're getting out of them or what we want others to do, our joy will die. People will disappoint us; they will fail us and we will fail them.

So how might this dance of enjoying others while also fighting sin look? For one thing, we can begin to view others the way the Lord does. God's declaration of humans, male and female, is that we are *all* made in his image. There's no distinction. What would happen if we started viewing others as God's created people? I think that's a good place to start. From there, if we remember that there are no mere mortals, as C. S. Lewis once wrote, we will know that all people need Jesus.[2] I know I need Jesus! This helps me to have grace for others. Yes, even grace for the awful racist comment that I received at my speaking event. We all need Jesus, and remembering that truth enables me to love, albeit imperfectly.

Perhaps another way to enjoy others is to relax. *Relax?* Yes, relax. Stop analyzing every friend and every move—if that's your temptation, as I know it is for many of us. To truly enjoy others is to let go and embrace them. No judging. No overanalyzing. Just enjoy. Please don't get me wrong; there's a time and place for evaluating friendships, and there's a good place for correcting our friends by speaking truth in love. But we ought not to feel guilty for simply sitting by a pool and chatting. Take in a movie. Grab dinner together. Sit around a table and talk. These aren't radical suggestions. They are incredibly simple, and yet I need to be reminded to simply relax with my friends at times.

Another way that we might enjoy others is to be the hands and feet of Jesus to them. That's one of those phrases that gets thrown around a lot, but basically it means that we can aim to meet the needs of others. When a woman comes home with a baby, perhaps you can bring her a meal. Maybe your single mom friend needs some girlfriend time and you could visit her at her home. I remember one day getting incredibly sick—actually my entire family was sick—and a friend brought us a meal of chicken noodle soup and rolls. She and I laugh about it now because she simply knocked on the door and left it on the porch so as not to get her own family sick, but, boy, was it a sweet gesture. She was showing love for me in a practical way, and not only did it bring me great joy and help, but I'd like to think she also received joy from that act of kindness.

So as we look to The Enjoy Project, don't be disappointed that it's not all about you. The goal for you and me is to learn what it *truly* means to enjoy. Maybe that looks like sending a friend a note of encouragement, making a call to someone you've been thinking about, saying yes to that invitation you've been putting off, or watching a movie with a loved one. Or maybe it's visiting that church member in the hospital, taking thirty minutes out of a hectic day to say hello to your neighbor, or telling your dear friend you love him or her.

The opportunities to invest in others are endless. Part of enjoying our relationships is making time for them. Pursue someone you'd like to know or someone you haven't seen in a while. Write

down ways your friends are meaningful to you. We are forgetful
people and need reminders of how great a gift our friends truly
are. At the same time, don't be discouraged if your pursuit and
intentionality are not reciprocated. What you and I are after is
changed hearts—our own. We may be rejected, but God is still
faithful. If you can remember this, then you can also rest easy as
you pursue people in love, knowing that your treasure and reward
are in heaven. God will be honored by your faithfulness.

No strategies will completely cause us to be free of relationship strife; we need Jesus! We also want to put our faith in action,
so we try, knowing that we will make mistakes and that God's
grace is essential in this quest. Part of this enjoyment is learning
what it means to glorify God in our relationships, and part of
glorifying God is acknowledging our desperate need for him.

The Enjoy Project:
The Gift of One Another

It's time to apply what you've read as you seek to enjoy your relationships.

1. Pray for someone who has offended you or who has been difficult to enjoy. List some of the ways God has gifted that individual for his glory.

2. Find a new way to encourage someone close to you, such as writing a note or calling just to express your appreciation for the specific ways that person is a gift of God for you.

3. Schedule a phone call, coffee date, or whatever works in your context with that one person you've been meaning to get together with.

4. Tell someone you love him. Get specific by describing exactly what you love about him.

5. Put away your phone, computer, work—whatever might be hindering you from engaging with friends and family—and intentionally spend an hour (or two or three!) doing something you all enjoy.

6. Look back over the chapter to identify one idea or truth that really stands out. Find a way to put that into practice this week.

7. Pray and preach the gospel to yourself.

Your kindness, Father, is so evidently seen in the gift of relationships. You created me to desire community and recognized my need for others. Yet I fall short of loving, serving, and caring for others as Christ has so clearly done for me. Thank you that I have a Savior who understands difficult and broken relationships. Help me to be quick to forgive and abound in love because of how you've first loved me.

True *biblical love*

is **compassionately**

and **righteously**

pursuing the

well-being

of another.

—Tony Evans

The Joy of Intimacy

When I was sixteen, I took a job at a local sports store. Little did I know at the time that God was providentially shaping the rest of my life.

My manager was a few years older than me. He was kind and flexible with my many extracurricular activities. I thought he was cute but never once thought I'd get to know him beyond asking if I could have yet another day off. I worked there for a few years before moving on to my next job. The summer after high school graduation a friendship seemed to develop between my former boss and me, and I decided I wouldn't mind getting to know him a little before college.

Our friendship grew from interest to care to romantic love. Neither of us were Christians, so our relationship was based mostly on attraction and personalities. We were the exact opposite, and I loved it. He was even keeled, introverted, thoughtful, business savvy, and maybe a little nerdy. I was more ambitious, excitable, and extroverted.

Eventually, he asked this young, spunky girl to be his bride. I was a college girl occupied with my own interests, and it wasn't the best timing. I wanted to see the world and do my own thing; he was older and wanted to settle down. Even so, I said yes, and then I later said no. We broke it off. And then we were dating again. Our relationship was all over the place. But then something happened that caused me to rethink everything.

A friend shared the gospel with me. She shared that I was a sinner in need of God's grace and that Jesus died on the cross bearing the wrath that I deserved. She explained it was a free gift, but she also noted that those who receive Christ repent—turn from their old ways. I resisted the idea of giving up my lifestyle. The truth had been planted and the seed was budding, but I wasn't ready to submit to Jesus. Instead, I continued in my roller-coaster relationship. We got engaged again, and then we broke it off again. This time I believed it was for good. The relationship seemed destroyed beyond repair.

I was left humbled by my sin in that relationship. I was humbled by my wandering heart. Tired of living for myself, I remembered the seed of Christ's love my friend had planted. I went to my friend's church, and that day I realized I wanted the Jesus my friend had been talking about. God worked a miracle of grace in my heart. At age twenty-two I was a new person—I could sense it to the core. And I couldn't wait to tell all my friends. I knew this meant the end of my relationship with my ex—possibly for good—since he was not interested in God.

A few years went by, and I invited him to a function. We barely spoke to each other, but when I saw him again, I knew that I loved him deeply. I had let go of any possibility of us getting back together. I was devoted to the Scriptures and wouldn't date a non-Christian. I actually didn't date at all, which was quite the change from my past priorities.

After a year I invited him to a function my church was sponsoring. Later that week he met with one of my guy friends, and God saved him. We both served in our local church, though in such different circles that we barely saw each other. I was serving in campus ministry, and he was involved in the singles ministry.

A year passed, and he asked if I'd consider dating. I said no. I was an intern at my church and didn't want the distraction of building a relationship. It was a tough year as I watched friends get engaged and begin relationships. Had I made the right choice? As I ministered to young college girls, I knew I'd made the right decision, but the possibility of him moving on was tough to accept.

But he didn't move on. And a year later, he asked me to go on a date. This time I said yes. Fast-forward to today, and I've been Thern's wife for thirteen years!

I share this not because it's a cute story of love lost and found again, but to highlight the amazing grace and redemption of our Lord and to help us begin to explore another good gift God created, one that's found in marriage. I think part of the reason my husband and I enjoy sexual intimacy is because we have invested first in our relationship. We've put in the time to grow together as a couple, and we've worked hard to build a strong marriage, grounded in Christ. I desire him because I'm with him, I know him, I know he loves me, and he is concerned deeply for me. We've failed miserably over and over again, but our relational bond and covenant before the Lord enable me to remember that he is a gift and our intimacy is a gift. So when I look at him, I'm compelled to touch him and fully express my love for him.

You can have a great relationship and not-so-great sex, but I don't believe you can have great sex without some sort of relationship. And as you'll see as we dive into this chapter, the goal isn't great sex but connected, enjoyable, delightful, even fun intimacy with your husband.

In this chapter I want you to think about *why* God designed us for the gift of sex. So often I think it's easy to get stuck on the how-tos without going deeper and understanding why God gave us this gift. So I don't intend to guilt you into having sex in your marriage. Instead, I want you to be encouraged and inspired, if you're a married woman, about this journey with your husband. And if you're single, I hope you will be encouraged about the way the Lord has fashioned your sexuality.

First, I'd like to help rescue sex from the dirty thing it's become. The topic of sex has been horribly tarnished by our world. But sex was created by God. We should declare this truth out loud (or to yourself if you're reading this in a crowded place). Go ahead and say it: "God created sex." This alone should bring a little relief to the strange, weird, and awful thing it's been transformed into. We shouldn't be embarrassed to talk about it. But I also know we have the reality of the Fall, which led to the corruption of sex. Sex is not dirty; we are. So it's not that we must change sex but rather that we must learn to change our thoughts and deeds to be like Christ so that we might truly enjoy this act God created.

Second, I want to avoid excluding a major part of our population. Most singles are created with a desire for sex. What does this mean if you're a single woman? If God doesn't withhold good from his people, how can you be encouraged while waiting? Whether you're single or married, I want you to be able to read this chapter and say "Amen!"

Third, I'd like to put sex in its place. I believe that the corruption I mentioned arises, at least in part, because sex can bring incredible and unexplainable pleasure. In short, it feels good, though

I realize this is not the case for everyone. As we'll see, God designed it to feel good, so it's not the feeling that's been corrupted but our hearts and minds as we experience it. We need to be reminded that sex is not the ultimate good. Sex is not the best that God has for us.

Men and women struggle with sexual sin because it seems better than what God has for them. Some believe human intimacy should fulfill their longings, and perhaps it does, for a moment. So instead of waiting, we go after what we think we want. A husband doesn't provide emotionally or relationally for his wife, so she seeks that fulfillment in another man. The sex may seem better because she feels a bond, but it is adultery. Perhaps you read the sentence "Sex is not the best that God has for us" in the previous paragraph and felt immediately justified in refusing sexual intimacy with your husband because you're just not that into it. That's just another way of saying you know better than God what's best for you. But that's not the answer either. We need to put sex in its rightful place, neither idolizing nor ignoring it.

GOD CREATED SEX

In the beginning, God created Adam and Eve, and one of his first commands was that a man would "leave his father and his mother and hold fast to his wife." The husband and wife would become one flesh (Genesis 2:24). One flesh—a commitment of intimacy from the beginning.

It's worth noting that this "one flesh" command was given before the Fall. God always intended for marriage to include sexual intimacy. Something else worth noting is that when God gave Adam and Eve to one another, they were naked and unashamed.

Author and physician Ed Wheat explained it this way:

> The ideal situation God intended for us is shown by the
> blissful words "they were both naked, the man and his
> wife, and were not ashamed" (Gen. 2:25). Adam and Eve
> could see each other as they really were, without shame,
> disappointment, or frustration. The sex relationship God
> had designed for them brought the blessings of compan-
> ionship, unity, and delight—and note that this was some
> time before the command to bear children was given
> (Gen. 3:16).[1]

God had the gift of marital intimacy in mind from the beginning. It was his gift to Adam and Eve. It is one of his many gifts
to you and me—in the proper context and at the proper time. It
is to be enjoyed and explored. The fact that, as God was creating
male and female, he included organs that would respond when
stimulated is amazing and intentional. He didn't have to create us
with these capabilities. He could have made us like plants, needing water and sunlight to grow. But he gave us each bodies. Sex
was intentionally created for our enjoyment.

Ultimately, as with everything in life, sex is designed to glorify God. If an orgasm is exhilarating, it pales in comparison to
the delight we will enjoy and experience when we are united with
our eternal husband. God describes the church as his bride (see
Ephesians 5:25–27). If we are his bride, then we can also know
that all the beauty and grace experienced in marital union reflects
how we will feel in the presence of our Savior. Sex is for our joy
and pleasure, but ultimately it is designed to remind us of our
union with Christ.

And it not only reflects how much love we will one day have for our Savior but also the great love Christ has for us right now. Jesus laid his life down, gave his life completely and fully, endured pain, sorrow, and, ultimately, the wrath of God on our behalf. His love is so much greater and purer than anything we could ever know on this earth; marriage is but a reflection of that ultimate sacrificial love shown to us by our Savior. Oh, what love! Amazing grace, how sweet the sound!

Sex is written about throughout the Scriptures, which clearly show that sex is indeed a gift, but one with boundaries and a context. God has made incredibly clear that sex outside of marriage is forbidden. We see this in numerous passages including, but not limited to Acts 15:20; 1 Corinthians 5:1; 6:13, 18; 7:2; 10:8; 2 Corinthians 12:21; Galatians 5:19; Ephesians 5:3; and the list goes on. In 1 Corinthians, Paul warns us to "flee from sexual immorality." He continues, "Every other sin a person commits is outside the body, but the sexually immoral person sins against his own body" (6:18). It's as if Paul is telling us, "Hey, this is actually hurting you as much as it's hurting others." He tells us to flee—to run for our lives.

We see a similar warning in Proverbs 5, which is dedicated to warning a young man against the temptation to adultery. Sexual sin is something most men and women believe they'll never fall into . . . until it's too late. Many of my girlfriends who have shared about their private battles tell me they're most often drawn into sexual sin not by overt sexual temptations but by their search for relational intimacy.

All forms of sexual sin are serious offenses to God. And here is what I know to be true: many of us have engaged in some form of sexual immorality. In fact, I don't know one person who hasn't.

Yet the amazing grace of God declares you and me righteous and pure before him because of the blood of the Lamb. No, we have not been faithful to him, but he will *always* be faithful to us. If you have committed sexual sin against God but have repented of this sin and are no longer walking in it, you must know there is now no condemnation for you. Rest in that forgiveness. We want to be like the woman caught in adultery—recipients of his forgiveness who then go and sin no more (see John 8:1–11).

It's astonishing, this grace God bestows on us. It's undeserved. As I heard someone say once, it's utterly uncalled for but it is true. God's grace covers all your past, present, and future sin—and, yes, this includes sexual sin. All our lust, desires for others, impure motives and sexual advances, and sexual intercourse outside the confines of marriage have been forgiven by the Lord; we have been bought with a price (see 1 Corinthians 6:20).

How do we respond to this amazing grace? We proclaim with Paul,

> Are we to continue in sin that grace may abound? By no means! How can we who died to sin still live in it? Do you not know that all of us who have been baptized into Christ Jesus were baptized into his death? We were buried therefore with him by baptism into death, in order that, just as Christ was raised from the dead by the glory of the Father, we too might walk in newness of life. (Romans 6:1–4)

We put off that old raggedy sin and walk in the newness of life. Even if that means today. Right now. Perhaps you are reading this and are caught in an ungodly relationship with a man or in fantasies or pornography. *Right now* you can run the other way. If you confess your sin, he is faithful and just to forgive you and purify you (see 1 John 1:9).

SEX AND THE SINGLE WOMAN

If sex is currently off-limits because you're single, divorced, widowed, or your husband is away for a period of time, does that mean that God is withholding one of his gifts from you? First, sex is a gift for this time on earth only. I have seen no evidence in Scripture that we will have sex in heaven. Marriage will also end (see Matthew 22:30). This matters because it confirms that sex isn't the *ultimate* gift from God. The ultimate gift from God is our true union with Christ for all time. You can be assured that if God is a loving Creator and loving Lord, he wouldn't withhold something unless doing so was ultimately for our good and his glory.

Before we move on, may I recommend the book *Sex and the Single Girl* by Ellen Dykas? She is a wise counselor and author and has been single her entire life. Here is a taste of what she has to say:

> The Bible clearly acknowledges our sexual appetites as part of the good way God created us, but God's Word does not assume that because the appetites are present they must be satisfied. This is because God understands the power of appetites that go unchecked by his standards for this expression. The Bible is extraordinarily candid about the power of sexual attractions and activity.[2]

And Dykas gives this encouragement specifically for single women:

> As single women, Jesus ultimately is not calling us to keep rules or lists of "don'ts," answer endless accountability questions, or say no to everything that feels precious to us. God *is* calling us to an ever-deepening relationship with him, enriched as we grow in wisdom through his Word.[3]

Isn't that what God calls all of us to? He calls us to a deeper relationship with himself. He calls us to remember that our forever is not in a relationship with a man but in our relationship with Jesus.

Sex, sexual desires, or even a lack of sexual desire should never define you and me. Our identity is in Christ. You can fight temptation. You can honor marriage and proclaim its goodness and gifts while remaining chaste.

When I think of someone who has lived this truth well, I can't help but think of Nancy DeMoss Wolgemuth. Nancy was single and celibate well into her fifties, content with her life until the Lord changed her heart and prepared a path for the man she would marry. In a recent interview after her wedding, Nancy shared with me, "When love is awakened in its time, it's to be enjoyed. Those who wait on the Lord will never be disappointed. What God gives me now is good and sufficient."[4]

This is not to say there's a promise of great sex simply because you wait. But as you wait, know that it is worth it. But even more, know that the Lord has already given you the ultimate gift, and it's not sex. He has given you Jesus.

Perhaps you, like many of my friends, have a desperate

longing to be married or you've had love but lost it. If so, I hope
Emily's story encourages your faith:

> It was close to Valentine's Day a few years ago, and I was
> perusing blogs. A few months prior, a relationship that I
> eagerly hoped would result in marriage, disintegrated and
> ended. I was left hopeful that God was working for my
> good but was saddened nonetheless. In the midst of that
> time, however, the thought struck me of a gift I had
> forgotten about.
>
> I was reminded that I had underappreciated the gift of
> singleness. The concept was not new; there were previous
> seasons in my life of excitement and contentment in
> singleness. While in this relationship that had just ended, I
> desired marriage. However, the best Gift-giver there is had
> mercifully given this gift of singleness to me for the display
> of His glorious grace. It was as though I were standing in
> line eagerly trying to trade it in for a gift I thought was
> better. I was willing to forfeit the joys of singleness on the
> altar of my own selfish ambition and ingratitude. Only
> God knows what is most beneficial for His children, and
> He would not withhold marriage if it were something
> needful.
>
> I received sweet grace that day! And there has been
> sustaining joy since that time. Marriage would be nice if
> the Lord should allow, but it is not a guarantee. I desire
> holiness, and I cannot be dependent on a man to satisfy
> longings that only God can meet. God gives good gifts
> (James 1:17), and He sovereignly provides or withholds
> things to aid in conformity to Jesus Christ (Romans 8). If

singleness is a means God uses for His glory and my joy, I want to gladly accept, cherish, and utilize the gift.[5]

WHEN THE GIFT FEELS LIKE A CURSE

I recently spoke with a Christian friend who all but hates sex with her husband. It is slightly miserable and feels like a task. I have another friend who cries after almost every sexual encounter with her husband. She's never been abused; she simply doesn't receive much pleasure from it, and so for her, too, it feels like a task. I've counseled and listened to countless women as they've worked through disappointment, discouragement, disgrace, and despair.

May I get personal? This has not been the case for me. I thoroughly enjoy intimacy with my man. That may be one reason my friends feel the freedom to ask me questions. I've definitely had to flee the temptation of lust, work through body image anxieties, and put away the sexual encounter ideal found in romantic comedies. It's not that our intimacy hasn't required work on my part. It's merely not the biggest struggle in my marriage. (There are others!)

That's one reason I'm excited to encourage you in this area. I'm not writing as a woman who has mastered marriage; unfortunately, I have sinned against my husband many times because of my lack of love and cherishing. I'm writing as a woman who enjoys physical intimacy but realizes that my sinful attitudes at times can affect that enjoyment.

Beyond issues of physical discomfort, I think one of the greatest hindrances to enjoying sexual intimacy with one's spouse is relational troubles. As I was studying, I found that Scripture often urges the man to enjoy his wife physically, so as not to be tempted by another woman. But women aren't addressed in the same way. As we noted earlier, sexual temptation for women seems to be tied to emotional desire more often than physical attraction.

One benefit of sexual intimacy is that as you and your husband become one, your hearts are being knit together.

I remember a heavy travel season for my husband. I missed him terribly, and though I enjoy the physical aspect of sexual intimacy, what I missed most during that time was the emotional closeness we experienced during intimacy. When he would get home from traveling, I remember desiring him so that we would *feel* close. Sexual intimacy creates a bond with another person that goes well beyond the physical. My husband and I are connected on so many levels, and there is a beautiful closeness in our relationship as we experience intimacy with one another.

Intimacy is more than sexual intercourse. Intimacy involves relationship.

However, as we explored in the previous chapter, the Fall has created a wedge between the man and woman that tends to twist the marital relationship. Here I'd like to concentrate on one particular issue: bitterness.

Have you ever struggled with forgiving your spouse or rehearsed an incident over and over again in your mind? Have you blamed him for your circumstance or lashed out? How about bringing up old hurts in an argument? These actions are evidence of bitterness.

Bitterness in its simplest form is unforgiveness. When you and I are bitter, we are holding on to something. In essence, we are holding sin against another. And bitterness can reach into the depths of our souls. The writer of Hebrews urges us: "Strive for peace with everyone, and for the holiness without which no one will see the Lord. See to it that no one fails to obtain the grace of God; that no 'root of bitterness' springs up and causes trouble, and by it many become defiled" (12:14–15).

I don't have a green thumb. I don't garden, though my daughter would like us to take it up as a family activity. But one thing I do know is that the roots of trees run quite deep—some as deep as twenty feet.[6] Therefore, it's incredibly difficult to dig up a tree. You and I couldn't go up to an oak tree and pull it out of the ground. It would take some device or machine to pull it up.

That's the trouble with bitterness. Its roots run deep. It hinders peace and distorts love. It blocks the grace of God from us—not that we wouldn't receive grace but that we wouldn't experience the freedom, joy, and peace that come from the grace of God. But before a root has an opportunity to grow deep, it starts as a seed. What you and I must do before the "bitter root" takes form is to remove the seed of unforgiveness. And if we fail to do that, we'll need the device of his power, grace, and the Holy Spirit to help us uproot and remove bitterness.

Here is a partial list of the evidences of bitterness, according to counselor Lou Priolo:[7]

- difficulty in resolving conflicts
- acts of vengeance
- withdrawal
- outbursts of anger
- biting sarcasm
- condescending communication
- criticism
- suspicion and distrust

- intolerance
- impatience
- disrespect

With this list in mind, think of times when you did not desire or respond to the sexual advances of your husband. Perhaps you were tired, but is there a chance it could be anything else? Or think about a time of intimacy that you wished away. Was it because of an argument? Were you perhaps resentful over words said or left unsaid, over actions you found hurtful or frustrating?

The Fall affects so much, doesn't it?

If your resistance to sexual intimacy with your husband is actually a product of bitterness, God has given you a way to put away bitterness through his Son. We have a command to love, even love our enemies (see Matthew 5:44). Maybe you view your husband as the enemy—but in reality, is he? Please know I'm not speaking here of the deep wounds left by infidelity or of the terrible circumstances of an abusive relationship. In those cases I would encourage you to seek the help of a biblical counselor. I'm referring instead to those ordinary, day-to-day troubles that produce bitterness if we focus on them. Maybe he won't pick up his socks. Or he seems more interested in what's on his phone than what's going on with the kids. Or he didn't fully appreciate your efforts in preparing the meal.

We must fight this bitter root by preaching to ourselves gospel truth about our husbands. He is forgiven as you are forgiven. He is clothed with righteousness as you are clothed with righteousness. He is dearly loved by God as you are dearly loved by God. His sins are as far as the east is from the west. Yours too! That's how we forgive—we remind ourselves of how much we've been forgiven. We extend to others the same grace God has extended to us.

Other Threats to Intimacy

Beyond bitterness, many other things can push sexual intimacy to the back burner.

If you have children, therein lies an unending list of distractions for sexual intimacy. Children are a joy and a gift, and, funny enough, sex is traditionally the way most children enter families. Yet children also take time and energy, which means we must get creative to make sure that time alone with our spouses isn't completely neglected.

Other hindrances include tiredness and plain old disinterest. Friends have shared with me that making time for sex isn't their trouble; it's becoming distracted and uninterested *while* having sex. With grocery lists, work projects, the family calendar, relational issues, and other concerns constantly whirling through their brains, women often find it difficult to shut out the world and focus on their husbands. The challenge is to create space in our minds and emotions to enjoy it. The goal would be to learn how to take captive our thoughts so we can be all there while we are intimate.

I'd like to encourage you, unless illness or other circumstances require abstinence from sex, that the pursuit of intimacy should be a priority in your marriage. Paul exhorted us in this challenge:

> "It is good for a man not to have sexual relations with a
> woman." But because of the temptation to sexual immo-
> rality, each man should have his own wife and each
> woman her own husband. The husband should give to his
> wife her conjugal rights, and likewise the wife to her

husband. For the wife does not have authority over her own body, but the husband does. Likewise the husband does not have authority over his own body, but the wife does. Do not deprive one another, except perhaps by agreement for a limited time, that you may devote yourselves to prayer; but then come together again, so that Satan may not tempt you because of your lack of self-control. (1 Corinthians 7:1–5)

These verses reveal so much. First, it's good to note that singleness is indeed a gift. "It is good for a man not to have sexual relations with a woman" because that means he can focus his energy and devotion on serving God. But if you aren't single, then Paul said each woman should own her husband's body and her husband owns hers. Some might cringe at the "ownership" language Paul used in these verses, but he's referring not to an oppressive relationship but to a wholehearted commitment to one's spouse. In my marriage, my body is not my own and neither is my husband's body his own. I think in using this language Paul paints a beautiful picture of the unity, both spiritual and physical, in marriage. We are so much "one" that our bodies aren't even our own. When I lie with my husband, I'm essentially telling him, I'm yours and you're mine. What beauty!

Another lesson that comes out of these verses is that we are often too confident in our strength. No one gets married thinking, *In five years I'll probably be sleeping with my neighbor.* Adultery isn't typically planned. And to be clear, even couples who consistently engage in sex are not immune to adultery. Sexual intimacy isn't a sure guard against sexual sin. Our sin originates from our hearts. Therefore, we want to kill the temptation as soon as it comes. Let's be wise when we sense ourselves drawn toward other men, whether physically *or* emotionally. Paul gave this warning for a purpose. Elsewhere, he also cautioned,

> Therefore let anyone who thinks that he stands take heed lest he fall. No temptation has overtaken you that is not common to man. God is faithful, and he will not let you be tempted beyond your ability, but with the temptation he will also provide the way of escape, that you may be able to endure it. (1 Corinthians 10:12–13)

We may have strong marriages, ones that are good and healthy. But if we think we are secure, if we begin to take liberties because we're confident in our own strength, we are putting our relationships at risk. We don't want to be paranoid, but we do want to be wise. Wisdom would say if you are physically able to engage in sexual intimacy but withhold your body because you don't feel like it, you may need to reevaluate your motives.

There are, of course, times when we must abstain or circumstances in which we are forced to abstain. What happens when one spouse or the other gets the flu? What if your husband experiences negative effects from treatment for prostate cancer? Or those six weeks after a pregnancy or when your husband is deployed? What if one of you is incapacitated for any reason? A marriage can surely glorify God without sexual intercourse. This is another reason we cannot make sex the ultimate gift and the only means of intimacy within marriage. But without a compelling reason to avoid sexual intimacy, those of us who are married are encouraged to enjoy this experience as a glorious gift from God.

I know I said this wouldn't be a "how to" chapter, but I would like to talk briefly about communication. Taking steps to better communicate and connect with your spouse could resolve much of your sexual intimacy struggles. Communication certainly has been key for my husband and me in relating to one another in all aspects of marriage. When we aren't communicating well, much about our relationship falls apart for a season, including sexual intimacy.

I don't want you to think communication is a magic pill. You could read this chapter and still remain unable to enjoy sex, because sexual intimacy takes two. But I do believe that intimacy between husband and wife begins with communication. Start there and pray that the Lord would give you and your husband the same vision for your marriage.

THE JOY OF BEING KNOWN AND LOVED

Besides warning us against sexual immorality, the Bible also celebrates sexual intimacy within the context of marriage. As I noted earlier, as I worked my way through Scripture, I realized that so many of the directives regarding sexual delight and joy are directed toward men. Verses like "Let your fountain be blessed, and rejoice in the wife of your youth. . . . Let her breasts fill you at all times with delight; be intoxicated always in her love" (Proverbs 5:18–19) and "How beautiful and pleasant you are, O loved one, with all your delights! Your stature is like a palm tree, and your breasts are like its clusters. I say I will climb the palm tree and lay hold of its fruit" (Song of Solomon 7:6–8).

But of course we know that women also can enjoy sexual intimacy, not only because of the way our generous God has created us, but also because, as the apostle Paul explained in 1 Corinthians, husbands *and* wives have a right to each other's bodies and any withholding by the man or woman should be done with mutual consent (see 7:1–5). Clearly sex is not intended for a man's desire only. Yet women sometimes feel strange or even sort of guilty for this desire. Please know that if you desire your husband, that's a good thing. It is from God, a part of his design.

This brings us back to where we started this chapter: sexual intimacy is a gift. My prayer for you, if you're a married woman, is that you would find ways to enjoy this good gift from God. If something is hindering your enjoyment, be it sin or an overly full schedule, ask the Lord to help you overcome those obstacles and enjoy this marital gift. If you are dealing with a physical issue that makes intimacy painful, please seek medical help. And if you're struggling with the effects of a past painful situation, such as sexual abuse or rape, I encourage you to seek counseling. This chapter is not meant to leave you feeling guilty but to give you hope that you can more fully enjoy this gift.

Sexual intimacy involves knowing and being known and expressing our love deeply. As a matter of fact, the Bible often uses this language of "knowing" to describe sex: "Adam knew Eve" (Genesis 4:1). You and I have the freedom to express intimate, knowing love in physical ways with our husbands. And not only do we get to express it but we also get to receive it.

There is something incredibly comforting and peaceful about being in the arms of my husband. I love him more deeply than I could ever have imagined. God is the only one who knows me more than my husband does. No other relationship on this earth is more binding and intensely familiar than that of my husband. There's such joy in the fact that I'm known and loved. He isn't my source of joy, but I do enjoy him and our love as a result.

At the same time, the joy of sexual intimacy is preserved and protected when we remember its proper place. We want to guard against making sex an idol, the *ultimate* thing in our relationship, or putting too much pressure on performing. When we do that, we strip away the enjoyment, and sex becomes a duty rather than a delight. Let's remember that sex is a gift to be enjoyed without pressure. Inevitably we will go through seasons when sex isn't easy, perhaps due to sickness or the exhaustion of a new baby or dealing with a crisis. But our marriages don't have to fall apart as a result. As we hold sex in its proper place, we can walk through those seasons without guilt and enjoy other forms of intimacy.

My prayer for you, if you are single, is that you would know that you are loved deeply by Jesus. He is your dearest friend, and you will one day be united with him forevermore. He is not withholding his best from you. If you long for the sexual intimacy that is reserved for marriage, I pray that the Lord would answer that desire in time. But if he doesn't, I pray you would be satisfied in the steadfast love of the Lord.

The Enjoy Project:
The Joy of Intimacy

Although this chapter is for all women, married or single, I thought I'd reserve this project for married women. If you are unmarried, you might consider these resources for further reading: *Sex and the Single Girl* by Ellen Dykas and *Divine Sex* by Jonathan Grant.

1. Think on what is true, noble, and pure regarding your spouse. Think of his godly characteristics, his gifts, the things you like most about him. Think of evidence of grace in his life.

2. Daydream—think about a recent time of intimacy with your spouse. This is not lust! It is remembering your husband and your joy together. Perhaps do this in anticipation of a time of intimacy this evening.

3. Plan a time of intimacy. This might mean taking the initiative. Remember that if you are unable to have sexual intercourse, intimacy can be a variety of things. Think about or write down how sexual intimacy increases your love and feelings of closeness to your spouse.

4. Reflect on your marriage with Christ. How can your anticipation of eternal enjoyment with Jesus help shape your temporary, earthly marriage? Reflect and, if possible, put some of the thoughts into action, perhaps by writing

your spouse a love letter or choosing to let go of something that has planted bitterness in your heart.

5. Know thyself: Think of reasons you don't prefer sexual intimacy with your husband. Aside from those things that require medical attention or the help of a counselor, how can you remove those barriers from your physical relationship with your spouse?

6. Look back over the chapter to identify one idea or truth that really stands out. Find a way to put that into practice this week.

7. Pray and preach the gospel to yourself.

God, sexual intimacy offers great potential for joy as well as for deep pain and confusion. Help me to keep this gift in its proper place, and guard me from the temptation to idolatry. Thank you that you've created me to so deeply enjoy this gift inside of marriage. And may this gift point me to the truth that I am deeply known and loved by you.

To be *loved* but not known

is comforting but superficial.

To be *known* and not loved

is our greatest fear.

But to be **fully known** and

truly loved is, well,

a lot like being

loved by God.

—Timothy Keller

Created to Work

I barely remember a day when I wasn't working. In middle school I started a bakery out of our house and sold pineapple upside-down cakes, pies, and other baked goods to area businesses. I still can't believe they bought items from a little girl baking out of her home. I even sold something for an office picnic! At that age I didn't understand supply and demand and as a result had to shut down my little business within a week. But it was an exciting week!

I already mentioned my high school job at a sports store. Before my son was born, I managed the sales department of a major fitness facility. After he was born, I decided to go back to work but on a part-time basis and only if I could bring him with me. I was a group fitness instructor and eventually managed a group of fitness instructors.

My primary work these days is that of a mother. I also write, speak, care for my home, and go to an office for a ministry twice a week. I work.

But working hasn't been easy. Besides the occasional relational difficulty with coworkers, there have been times I simply don't care to work or other times I've become a workaholic for a season. Honestly, I've only just begun to understand the great balance between work and rest, which I'll cover in the next chapter, and it's due in large part to writing this book! I share this so you know I'm in the fight along with you as we discover how to delight in work even when it's hard!

LABOR PAINS

An abundance of faith and work networks have emerged over the past few years. I think it's an encouraging indication that the church is realizing the importance of work—that all of life matters to God. In the Creation account, we see that God worked for six days and then rested. For six days he displayed his awesomeness by creating water, plants, animals, light from the darkness, day and night, the heavens and earth, and man. He was thoughtful in his design. Each intricate detail was developed with care. God didn't cut corners or skip a day; he worked diligently and perfectly to create the world and all that would inhabit it. And when he was done with that work, he rested.

It's important to note that God does not sin—he is completely righteous. Therefore, we can conclude that work is not sinful nor is it a result of sin. *God* worked, right from the start! Author and pastor Tim Keller said, "God worked for the sheer joy of it. Work could not have a more exalted inauguration."[1] And not only did God work but he also placed man in the garden and instructed him to work it and keep it—*before* the Fall (see Genesis 2:15). Work is a part of God's design for his creation.

We find further confirmation of this in Jesus. Jesus, the God-man, worked as a carpenter (see Mark 6:3). And we know that

Jesus, too, is perfect, completely righteous. He is not capable of sinning. This is yet another reason we can be reassured that work, in and of itself, is not sinful, nor is it a result of the Fall.

As we delve into the theology of work, we'll see that it's another of God's good gifts, meant to be enjoyed.

But there's a problem.

The problem is always the same—sin.

When sin came into the world, it didn't change the nature of work but our response to work. We often think of work as a necessary evil. We go about grumbling as each hour of our workday ticks by. We may resent work because of laziness, which also leads to despair. Other times we are so devoted to work that everything else is neglected—family, church, and even health take a backseat. Work becomes an idol, where we try to find our complete joy, satisfaction, and identity. This is true not just of paid employment but even in our household work or the responsibilities of parenting. We struggle with great discontentment in our work, believing we aren't getting the recognition we deserve or resenting tasks we believe are beneath us, to name a few possible reasons. Or we feel defeated when we believe we're failing.

Work, like all good things, has been marred by the Fall. We feel the reality of the curse daily as we labor. God said to Adam,

> Because you have listened to the voice of your wife and have eaten of the tree of which I commanded you, "You shall not eat of it," cursed is the ground because of you; in pain you shall eat of it all the days of your life; thorns and thistles it shall bring forth for you; and you shall eat the plants of the field. By the sweat of your face you shall eat bread, till you return to the ground. (Genesis 3:17–19)

This is terrible and sad news. God had abundantly provided for Adam's needs. He didn't have to worry about laboring to eat—he would simply eat as much as he liked. His labor was pure joy and delight. It was a privilege that God would allow him to work the land he had created. Now, because of the Fall, all of us must work for food. And we don't only work; we work hard and we sweat. It's laborious. And if we don't have the proper perspective, it can be downright dreadful. We may resonate with the words of Ecclesiastes: "Vanity of vanities, says the Preacher, vanity of vanities! All is vanity. What does man gain by all the toil at which he toils under the sun?" (1:1–3).

Well, isn't that motivating? Vanity. It is all vanity . . . *if* it's all about you and me. It is all vanity . . . *if* we don't realize our labors are meant to draw attention to and glorify God. And isn't it amazing that we can bring God glory even in mundane tasks? Isn't it amazing that God delights in the work of a sanitation engineer as much as in the work of a pastor? Keller put it this way: "All work has dignity because it reflects God's image in us, and also because the material creation we are called to care for is good."[2]

When you and I work, we reflect some aspect of our Creator God. For the mother laboring to care for the needs of her children—how much more does God provide for every need of his children? For the woman designing a logo for a company—God created blue betta fish out of nothing. For the woman sitting at her desk organizing the operations for the day—scientific laws and the order of the universe come from God. Work is about God, reflects God, and can glorify God.

Whether you're tilling the ground for a vegetable garden to feed people or a flower garden to bring beauty, you are caring for God's creation and for his people. In many ways, our work has value because it benefits others. And God invites us to partner with him and participate in the ongoing activities of God in this world. What a joy, honor, and privilege work has the potential to be.

I once heard a pastor say that the only vocation that won't be in heaven is his because we will not need to have the Word preached to us—we'll see clearly and will be with our great Shepherd. Our work is significant and good, but we find the greatest freedom to enjoy work in understanding that our satisfaction and joy can only be derived from and through Jesus.

THE BEAUTIFUL MUNDANE

One of the hardest aspects of work, besides finding a balance with rest, which I'll get to in the next chapter, is how mundane and repetitive so much of it is. The work of motherhood can be exciting as we guide our children in learning to walk and read and love the Lord, but day to day it involves countless menial tasks. Nailing a presentation at the office can surely be motivating, but hours upon hours of sitting at a desk can drain your enthusiasm. Helping customers find just what they are seeking can be satisfying, but stocking shelves may leave you feeling like a robot. The truth is, *any* work at some point becomes mundane because it's not meant to be completely fulfilling. At some point, you and I will likely battle feelings of boredom or question the worth of the work we do.

Here's a glimpse of the reality of my days when my children were younger: It's six o'clock in the morning, and my two-year-old and five-year-old continue to sleep as I ease gently into a chair and break open my Bible. Even the slightest noise might wake my youngest, and once that happens, it's time to get to work. After they wake, I'm left wondering what in the world I will do all day with them.

Each day I would wake up and have the task of figuring out how to teach, play with, and lovingly serve two small children. To say it was easy would be a lie. Young children are highly unpredictable, full of energy, and at times fussy. They need our constant attention, energy, and care. The question I wrestled with was what to do with the mundane, everyday sameness that characterizes so much of work. How could I find joy in washing dishes for the third time that day?

This problem isn't unique to the work of motherhood. Some days now, as I work to finish up a project, all I can think about is how long it is until the next break or vacation. I grow frustrated when I'm misunderstood or when I misunderstand others. I can get lonely during long hours of solitude while writing. My to-do list can seem endless, and instead of focusing on my limitations and God's sustaining grace, I become anxious and worried. Every day isn't like this, but there are too many that are.

I know I'm not alone in struggling to consistently view work as a gift.

One day as my husband prepared to walk out the door for work, our daughter began to cry. When she was a toddler, that was a normal scene in our home. This particular day stands out to me not because she cried but because he did. I have always been aware that leaving to spend the majority of his day at work, away from us, would never be his preference, but the significance of Thern's sacrifice struck me deeply. He works a normal work week, averaging forty-five or more hours per week. When he arrives home, he has approximately four hours each night to spend with us, two of which are taken up by eating and preparing our children for sleep.

My husband works to serve our family and to serve the Lord. He feels a calling to work. He believes it is his God-given responsibility. As we've already explored, work was established before the Fall. In the garden, God supplied work for men and women.

It is good that we work. It is good that my husband works. But it does require a sacrifice, and I don't want to minimize the tough parts of work even as we seek to enjoy it. We spend most of our hours working, so we must learn to enjoy it, to reclaim it from the effects of the Fall and ultimately to bring God glory through our efforts.

God's words help motivate us to work: "Whatever you do, work heartily, as for the Lord and not for men, knowing that from the Lord you will receive the inheritance as your reward. You are serving the Lord Christ" (Colossians 3:23–24). Have you ever thought of your everyday work as serving the Lord? It's hard to imagine that sending e-mails, picking up mail, writing letters, serving food at a restaurant, or scrubbing toilets could be work that actually serves the Lord, but here Paul tells us otherwise. We work heartily not to please our bosses, our children, our spouse, or our coworkers; we work for the Lord. And remarkably, there's a reward awaiting us.

A WORD TO MOMS

Motherhood is often called a labor of love. It's a job that doesn't receive a paycheck but has sweet rewards. It's filled with ordinary tasks like grocery shopping, picking up kids, teaching them, and doing the same thing again the next day and the day after that. It can often feel as if your work isn't appreciated, and at times you may wonder if it matters at all, if any of your efforts make a difference.

John Piper, in his book *Risk Is Right,* asserted that a life unwasted is a life that honors Christ, magnifies Christ, and makes much of Christ. He went on to say,

> There are a thousand ways to magnify Christ in life and death. None should be scorned. All are important. But none makes the worth of Christ shine more brightly than sacrificial love for other people in the name of Jesus. If Christ is so valuable that the hope of his immediate and eternal fellowship after death frees us from the self-serving fear of dying and enables us to lay down our lives for the good of others, such love magnifies the glory of Christ like nothing else in the world.[3]

I can think of no better description of what we do every day as mothers. A mom who serves her children through menial tasks, shares her faith, and presses into Christ to know him more sounds like a mom committed to sacrificial love for other people. This is true for the stay-at-home mom, the work-at-home mom, and the mom who, like mine did, works hard during the day at her nine-to-five job so that her children will be able to eat and have a chance at a future, and then comes home to continue lovingly serving her family with her hands in practical ways and with her knees on the ground in prayer. Mothers of all styles, various practices, and a range of gifting work hard for others daily and, in the process, glorify God with their actions.

You and I both know the losses associated with motherhood.

You lose sleep. Your body is put through the wringer to give birth or your heart is squeezed tight through the long process of adoption. You lose certain freedoms because sweet little lives are dependent upon you. You lose the opportunity to nibble chocolate without sharing (or at least hiding) and the privilege of using the bathroom in peace. I'm not even going to think about what we lose in the teenage years!

Because of the potential and real losses that are a part of motherhood, this labor of love can be difficult to enjoy at times. I think we mothers do each other a disservice if we pretend that every moment of every day is filled with wonder and excitement and joy. It's hard. It's work. It's good, hard work. This work must be shored up by something other than sentimentalism. Thankfully, we can turn to the Word of God for help and an adjustment to our vision.

We know that "whoever would save his life will lose it, but whoever loses his life for my sake will find it" (Matthew 16:25). Therein lies the crux of our loss. As Christian moms, we lose not for our sake and really not even for the sake of our children but for the sake of Christ. We live to Christ and we die to Christ. It is for his sake and glory that we give our lives to the service of child rearing. Like Paul we say, "But whatever gain I had, I counted as loss for the sake of Christ. Indeed, I count everything as loss because of the surpassing worth of knowing Christ Jesus my Lord. For his sake I have suffered the loss of all things and count them as rubbish, in order that I may gain Christ" (Philippians 3:7–8).

Our loss—of comfort, time, energy, opportunity—isn't a loss at all. It's a gain! Because our gain as a result of sacrifice is Christ. Less of us, more of him. That is a wonderful exchange.

We can take joy in knowing that our efforts, when made out

of love for Jesus and our children, bring glory to God. I'm talking to *all* moms: The mom who is making a valiant effort to show Christ to her children. The mom who puts food on the table and labors to love. The mom who wipes noses and kisses boo-boos. The mom who washes the sports jersey and drives to piano lessons. And, yes, the mom who labors in her home, often alone and unnoticed, without fanfare. You don't have to go to China to give your life for Christ. *Lay down your life and you will find it.*

Enjoying Work

Whatever your workday involves—whether slicing up apples for small people, creating spreadsheets, engaging with customers, or juggling multiple roles—you might be asking, *How can work be a joy and delight when it's also mundane and requires sacrifice?*

For me in those early years of motherhood, the answer started with remembering that my children are a gift from God and then planning our days. Isn't that true of all our work? If we can begin to see our work as a gift rather than a curse, it's much easier to enjoy, even in the difficult times. And to take it a step further, if we see our work as working for the Lord—whatever you do, do it for his glory—then what great joy and motivation that would produce in us.

Another key to enjoying work is *learning* to be content. As we saw in chapter 1, Paul, who by earthly standards had every reason to be discontent, said he had learned to be content in whatever circumstance (see Philippians 4:12–13). He wasn't born content. He didn't receive his first imprisonment and think to himself, *This is wonderful!* Paul had to learn to be content with plenty and with nothing.

We too must learn to be content as we work. Although our jobs can definitely be satisfying, they'll never fill a void or be completely fulfilling in every aspect. We must fight for contentment in our labors.

Please note that this chapter is not about calling. You may be called to many things, none of which relate to how you currently make your living. I wish I had a magic button to tell you what to do. There are volumes of books that speak to calling, but my desire is to help you enjoy the work the Lord has given you for today. Even if we aren't sure of our calling, we know we are called to work. And if we look for opportunities to do that work to the glory of God and for the sake of helping others, we will find joy along the way.

FRUITFUL LABOR

Think about the ambitions, goals, and dreams you might have for serving the Lord for the benefit of the body of Christ. Now consider why you might not be pursuing them. Perhaps you don't share your vision with others who could help because you don't want to appear proud. Maybe you have an idea for writing an article that might build the faith of others, but you fear your submission will be rejected. Or maybe you have an idea for a business but the thought of taking that entrepreneurial risk paralyzes you.

There are risks to running the race set before us, risks in trusting the Lord with our pursuits. But we find joy in work when we step up to challenges rather than hiding in our comfort zones. When you recognize that you've been holding back out of fear of failure or because of worry about giving in to pride, you can find peace in God's Word that you are forgiven and then run hard for

Christ. Let's not allow fear to stifle our service or our passion for meeting needs. Fear twists the gospel by saying Jesus's finished work on the cross was enough for our salvation but *not* enough for us to finish the race. That's not what the Word of God says. Rather, "his divine power has granted to us all things that pertain to life and godliness, through the knowledge of him who called us to his own glory and excellence" (2 Peter 1:3). Because of Jesus, we have access to power through the Spirit.

I'm not writing as someone who seems to have it all figured out. I'm with you in wondering about the danger of pride mixed with ambition as we pursue business and ministry ventures. But I find comfort in knowing that God can help us join Paul in saying, "For to me to live is Christ, and to die is gain. If I am to live in the flesh, that means fruitful labor for me" (Philippians 1:21–22). Your labor for the Lord may look drastically different from mine, but our ambition can indeed be gospel centered. As Paul said, "I make it my ambition to preach the gospel, . . . [so that] 'those who have never been told of him will see, and those who have never heard will understand'" (Romans 15:20–21). We too can make it our ambition to preach the gospel wherever we are.

Having an ambition for the gospel pushes us to do things we never expected. It incites us to look beyond the borders of our comfort and convenience. The gospel stokes ambition by making audacious claims upon it. We can pursue all sorts of work with the end of glorifying Jesus in mind. We can also know that our presence in our jobs goes far beyond merely carrying out the tasks of the day. We are ambassadors of Christ. We are in the world but not of the world. We have an opportunity to be a shining light to those around us and, Lord willing, to share Jesus with those near us. We can boldly and determinedly, without fear, proclaim Christ in this world through the work we're doing—any kind of work.

But we still have to fight against sin so we might enjoy our work. That struggle is real.

ALL TO THE GLORY OF GOD

Perhaps your struggle is not in finding ambition to pursue new ventures but in finding motivation to continue the work you're doing. God, who created work, also created a way of escape from our sinful tendencies to either fight against working or to make work an idol. Jesus provides the grace to delight in the work he has given us to do.

In their helpful book *The Gospel at Work,* authors Sebastian Traeger and Greg Gilbert explained how this grace shapes our approach to work:

> You are free, not to make your work into an idol, but to make it an arena for loving God and loving others. You're free from the trap of idleness, from growing frustrated and bitter in the difficulties or drudgery your job brings. Your happiness is secured elsewhere; you don't have to be discouraged that your job isn't providing it.[4]

We are free to work to the glory of God! All work is meant to ultimately point to the Creator, who provides the work we do. God worked, and he invites us to work as we participate along with him in activities that ultimately reflect our Creator God. You and I can begin to delight in our work by intentionally recognizing that it is God who has given us that work. So whether we are serving up school lunches or negotiating mergers, our work is important to God and provides opportunities to reflect his creativity, order, and beauty. Our enjoyment of work doesn't so much rely on ourselves as much as it relies on our point of view. We work to bring God glory. We work because God has given us various skills that are useful and because he has instructed us to work. Keeping these truths in mind helps us avoid corrupt work practices and negative attitudes about our roles.

Jesus came to serve and not be served (see Matthew 20:28). Our aim and goal is to reflect him in all we do, including work. When we look to God as our provider, when we remember that we matter to God and our work matters to God, then we find delight and joy in serving and loving others through our work. This is what it means to keep work in its proper place.

Traeger and Gilbert eloquently explained,

> You are now free. Free from the need to secure self-worth
> through performance. Free from the fear you will lose
> what is most precious to you if things don't go well. Free
> from a mad dash to work, work, work without any
> rest—as if the world depended on your effort. Free to
> work before the King with joy, even if it's not the work you
> would have chosen for yourself. Free to serve others as you
> worship the King.[5]

The gospel affects all of life, doesn't it? The good news that Jesus died for our idolatry and our laziness gives us the power to enjoy work and find our satisfaction in Jesus. We can't work apart from this knowledge and also glorify God in our work. To work as unto the Lord means to work knowing that everything we do, every effort, has been bought by the blood of Jesus. Every failure has been paid for already. Jesus is our righteousness, no matter what. That's good news to the weary worker bee!

You can be encouraged in your work not because you scored a great deal, though that may be worth celebrating, but because you have the privilege to do this work for Jesus and because God is glorified in your efforts.

And this earthly work doesn't have the final word. Jesus made a promise: "My food is to do the will of him who sent me and to accomplish his work" (John 4:34). He delights to finish his good work that he began.

One day, all will once again be perfect. We will be restored to the pre-Fall state, in the garden, working with joy and delight for eternity. "No longer will there be anything accursed, but the throne of God and of the Lamb will be in it, and his servants will worship him" (Revelation 22:3).

Amen.

The Enjoy Project:
Created to Work

1. Let's be honest; most work can seem or actually be mundane. Few of us are professional athletes or jump out of planes for a living. Even so, think of one or two things you can change in your workday to make it more enjoyable, such as taking a walk or meeting a friend for lunch instead of working at your desk. Now go and do it.

2. List the various types of work that fill your days, such as work for a paycheck, preparing meals, gardening, or caring for an ailing loved one. Now list ten reasons you love your work. If *love* is too strong a word, maybe there are a few things you like or appreciate about your work? Then tape the reasons to your computer screen or dashboard or keep them in a notebook as a reference.

3. List five reasons you do not enjoy your work. (Notice it's a smaller list.) Now ask yourself why. Is there anything you can do to change these things? Could you seek to resolve a conflict, schedule a discussion with your boss about the work environment, or simply adjust your attitude by addressing a worry or bitterness that has taken root in your heart? If you can take any action to make changes in these areas, go ahead.

4. What might be depleting your energy or hindering you from getting things done? Consider some ways to make your work more efficient, such as planning your day the night before or organizing your desk.

5. Part of enjoying work involves stopping—as in closing down to reenergize for a new day. In the next chapter we'll explore the concept of rest, but if you find it difficult to turn off work, this is your chance to get a head start. Simply take a break. Shut down your computer, turn off your phone, and choose to occupy your mind with something else—that's your action step.

6. Look back over the chapter to identify one idea or truth that really stands out. Find a way to put that into practice this week.

7. Pray and preach the gospel to yourself.

Father, when you created humanity, you gave us work to do to steward the world you made. Thank you for giving me gifts and abilities that allow me to work in unique ways. As I work, help me to keep my focus on you. I don't work to receive the praise of those around me; I work to and for your glory. And my work isn't to earn your favor or love or acceptance; I know those things come only through the grace that has saved me.

No **work** is insignificant.

All **labor** that uplifts humanity

has *dignity*

and *importance*

and should be undertaken with

painstaking

excellence.

—Martin Luther King Jr.

The Freedom to

Press Pause

My friend was tired, all the time. But she couldn't put her finger on the reason for her desire to flee everything. As a homeschooling mother to five young children, involved in her church and dedicated to her friends, there was more going on in her life than she realized. She soon came to hate everything about it. Her marriage began to buckle under the weight of her jam-packed schedule that left little time for meaningful communication, her desire to be with her children suffered greatly, and she resented church as just another thing she *had* to do. She wanted to quit everything. I didn't blame her. But quitting wasn't the answer, although she probably did need to thin out some activity. Beneath that desire to flee and the compounding frustrations in her life was a deep fatigue. What she really needed was space to rest and play.

Does any of this sound familiar? Do you resonate with the fatigue and lack of margin that characterized my friend's life?

I wish I could say I close my eyes each night excited to rest or I look with eagerness and excitement on evenings when I have a lot to do but my kids want to play. The truth is, there's always so much to be done. There are dishes to wash and laundry to sort, an e-mail to respond to, the article due, and it just keeps coming. The work never ends. Despite organizers and apps and calendars to keep up with it all, it can seem nearly impossible. Some days I feel I've become a slave to the needs of others and to my own desire to check items off my to-do list.

But I find freedom in acknowledging that I simply can't do it all and that rest is essential if I'm going to do anything well.

The psalmist cautioned us:

Unless the LORD builds the house,
    those who build it labor in vain.
Unless the LORD watches over the city,
    the watchman stays awake in vain.
It is in vain that you rise up early
    and go late to rest,
eating the bread of anxious toil;
    for he gives to his beloved sleep. (Psalm 127:1–2)

Rest reminds me that unless the Lord builds the house, my labors are in vain. If I'm working like crazy but am filled with anxiety and fear, then my labors are meaningless. Rest is a gift from God to me as his beloved. When I don't take advantage of it, when I work all hours because I'm worried about getting things done, I'm actually being selfish by God's standards. Who would think that *not* resting was actually selfish?

I'm learning how to rest, and it's so freeing. What a relief to admit that only God can efficiently and effectively work twenty-four hours a day without rest.

Our bodies and minds aren't designed to keep going and going, like the Energizer Bunny. In fact, periods of rest allow for better, more productive periods of work.

PRESSING PAUSE

Before we dive into what hinders us from enjoying rest, I thought it would be helpful to define what I mean by rest. For our purposes, rest is pausing to refresh and rejuvenate our bodies and to renew our spirits. So we will be considering physical rest, namely, sleep or leisurely activity away from whatever you would define as work. We will also explore what it looks like to play, a fine art of children but one that adults tend to neglect. And we will examine why spiritual rest is vital if we're to truly enter into rest.

As we consider rest together, please keep in mind that certain activities you find restful others might consider work. For example, I have a friend who finds laundry to be completely relaxing, while I find laundry to be a product of the Fall! For some, resting is sitting on the porch with an open book; for others, it's relaxing with family and friends. For me, resting is grabbing my bike and cycling through the beautiful, rolling Tennessee terrain. How we rest will look different for each one of us. I will trust that you can identify what is work for you and what is rest.

While our bodies need a certain amount of sleep each night to function properly, we also are designed to take longer periods of rest, times when our activities are not centered on accomplishment. Such a day of rest is called a Sabbath—a day designated for solemn rest. A Sabbath isn't officially observed in our culture, but many use

Saturday or Sunday as their day of rest. Those whose roles at church require them to work on Sundays may take Monday as their Sabbath. Setting aside an entire day to rest isn't something we've made up; it's a part of the fabric of who we are and how we were made.

God created the earth and then rested on the seventh day (see Genesis 2:3). God, who needs no sleep, chose to rest, and as his image bearers made to reflect aspects of him, we also are created to rest. As a matter of fact, God thought rest was so important that he made it one of the Ten Commandments:

> Remember the Sabbath day, to keep it holy. Six days you
> shall labor, and do all your work, but the seventh day is a
> Sabbath to the LORD your God. On it you shall not do any
> work, you, or your son, or your daughter, your male servant,
> or your female servant, or your livestock, or the sojourner
> who is within your gates. For in six days the LORD made
> heaven and earth, the sea, and all that is in them, and rested
> on the seventh day. Therefore the LORD blessed the Sabbath
> day and made it holy. (Exodus 20:8–11)

No one and nothing was supposed to labor on the Sabbath. Even the animals were off the hook! That's pretty remarkable, and it's actually rather kind of the Lord. Rest should be refreshing and replenish us for the work ahead. But maybe you think rest is punishment rather than a gift. Tim Keller has some challenging words for us who seem to never stop working:

> Anyone who cannot obey God's command to observe the
> Sabbath is a slave, even a self-imposed one. Your own
> heart, or our materialistic culture, or an exploitative

organization, or all of the above, will be abusing you if you don't have the ability to be disciplined in your practice of Sabbath. Sabbath is therefore a declaration of our freedom. It means you are not a slave—not to your culture's expectations, your family's hopes, your medical school's demands, not even to your own insecurities. It is important that you learn to speak this truth to yourself with a note of triumph—otherwise you will feel guilty for taking time off, or you will be unable to truly unplug.[1]

Perhaps you are thinking, *Yes, but the law has been fulfilled, and we no longer* must *observe a Sabbath.* Observing a Sabbath, a day of rest, is not being chained down and oppressed by the law. It's quite the opposite. When we choose to rest, we express our dependence and trust in God. Rest frees us from the crazy busyness we often find ourselves in. It allows time for other things and people. And as Keller noted, we have freedom from guilt when we rest in this way because it's a command from our Lord.

Resting and observing a Sabbath does not equate to laziness. We've been sold a lie, perhaps wrapped up in the American Dream, that says we must go, go, go when God says we must rest. I hope in this chapter to challenge us to learn to rest and see the benefits of it and to work to create margin in our busy lives for this good gift from God. My prayer is that we would be free to rest *and* enjoy it.

Warning Against Idleness

The call to rest is not, however, an invitation to idleness. As we saw in the previous chapter, we sometimes mistakenly view work as a curse and, as a result, we idolize rest and play.

I've certainly experienced times when I wasn't eager to work. I've sat at my computer playing solitaire rather than writing an article or scrolled through social media instead of folding the laundry. Those Like buttons aren't going to push themselves, people!

It's like the cult classic *Ferris Bueller's Day Off*. (Wow, I just dated myself.) The lead character, Ferris Bueller, didn't want to go to school. So he faked an illness and dragged his girlfriend and his best friend into a day of teenage mischief. It seemed a fun escape from reality, but the adult in me now knows that he should have been at school. (Yep, I've dated myself.)

But rest is a gift that points us to God, not a goal in and of itself. To truly grasp the good in it and to experience the fullness of it, we must make sure that rest is in its proper place.

Paul strongly warned the Thessalonian church to steer clear of brothers who were idle, intentionally shirking their God-given responsibilities (see Genesis 2:15). Some individuals within the Thessalonian church were not only neglecting their work but also taking advantage of the kindness of the other members of the church and meddling in the affairs of the other Christians. Paul didn't mince words in his rebuke: "If anyone is not willing to work, let him not eat. For we hear that some among you walk in idleness, not busy at work, but busybodies" (2 Thessalonians 3:10–11). Ouch, Paul.

Clearly, idleness is a serious offense. God commands us to work, and it is important and necessary. So we want to watch out for slothful and lazy tendencies. But let's not confuse laziness with genuine rest, as God designed us to enjoy it.

WORK NEVER ENDS

Perhaps the greatest assault to our rest is a lack of margin—being overcommitted and busy. We also may wrestle with the sense that rest and relaxation are a waste of time. Remember the story I shared about buying my bike and then needing to find a "legitimate" purpose for it? Why is it so difficult to turn off and unplug? Just as it takes faith to believe in God's existence, it takes faith to believe he is in control of all our labors and the bottom line. It takes faith to rest.

I'll be honest; I have a love/hate relationship with rest. I know I need it, but so often I look at all that needs to be done and I just keep going and doing. And when I do rest, it can end in guilt—*I should have been working, but I chose to rest. What was I thinking when there's so much that needs to be done?* That's why I've been so eager to study about rest.

Like my friend whose story I shared at the beginning of this chapter, we are busy. We are busy chasing, perhaps chasing the American Dream of comfort and wealth and happiness. But as we have seen in historical events like the stock market crash leading to the Great Depression and the more recent Great Recession, the American Dream can be lost in a matter of minutes. But still we pursue it, and the chase leaves us restless, anxious, worried, and tired. The average American in full-time employment works an average of forty-seven hours per week.[2] By contrast, countries like France and Spain take full afternoon breaks as part of their cultural lifestyle. As a matter of fact, Americans work more than anyone in the industrialized world, retire later, and take fewer vacations.[3]

As we saw in the previous chapter, work is a good gift, but when misused or misunderstood, it becomes an idol that leads us on an endless chase for money, comfort, and security.

The Danger of Self-Sufficiency

Several times in my life, I've realized I was struggling with the big *S* word: self-sufficiency. Okay, maybe that's two words, but go with me. The Merriam-Webster dictionary defines *self-sufficient* as "able to maintain oneself or itself without outside aid: capable of providing for one's own needs." Though I see evidence of my attempts to be self-sufficient in many areas, it's most pronounced in my sleep habits. I'm often tempted to stay up to get things done or even watch a movie rather than go to sleep.

I believe self-sufficiency is at the root of our aversion to rest. Paul said, "Not that we are sufficient in ourselves to claim anything as coming from us, but our sufficiency is from God" (2 Corinthians 3:5). And we know that apart from Jesus we can do nothing (see John 15:5). Yet how often do we try?

The temptation of self-sufficiency can be difficult to recognize and even more difficult to resist. There's always work to be done, so how can we know whether our efforts are about getting things done or about getting them done apart from God's strength? Evaluating our habits and our attitudes may help us identify self-sufficiency. Do we feel rundown, irritable, frustrated, or anxious? Are we spending more time in worry than in prayer?

God made you and me to need sleep. I don't know about you, but something happens when I don't get enough. I often get sick, I'm irritable and impatient, and I can be weak and sluggish. You get the picture, and the picture isn't pretty! The solution is simple:

put down the pen or turn off the computer and lie down to sleep. When I do this, I almost always wake up with a clearer mind and an eagerness to start the day. It makes my work, housework, and writing time much more efficient. Plus, I just feel better.

There is only One who doesn't sleep (see Psalm 121:4). The rest of us are only fooling ourselves if we think we can be sustained for long without it. God designed us to need sleep so we could remember that we need him and that we aren't him! The truth is, I am the exact opposite of self-sufficient. I am unable to maintain myself without the aid of God's strength and the help of his Spirit (see Philippians 4:13). I am unable to provide for my own needs (see James 1:17). I need sleep. I need God.

As we've seen in Psalm 127:2, God gives sleep to his beloved. Sleep is a gift from God. Sleep reveals our deep need and dependence on God.

Maybe you aren't tempted to work long hours but you struggle to calm your mind to rest and sleep. You find yourself lying awake at night and replaying a situation over and over again in your head. You can't stop thinking about that conversation you had earlier. Or a deadline is looming and you worry you won't make it. Or you're mulling over how to mend a fractured relationship. Whatever it is, it robs you of joy, peace, and, ultimately, rest in the form of sleep and relaxation.

Certainly worry and anxiety are not the only things that rob us of sleep. Perhaps you suffer with insomnia, illness, or chronic pain. Some of these things are unfortunate results of living in a fallen world. Our only hope is to cry out to our Lord for healing and grace.

But if there isn't something outside your control that hinders you from rest, it may very well be a problem within you. This is where spiritual rest comes in.

SPIRITUAL REST

Hard work turns a profit. That's what we are used to; it is the economy by which we live. We know that our labors earn us something, so we toil. But the economy of the spiritual realm couldn't be further from what we're accustomed to in the workforce. Our labors for the Lord are not to earn his favor. If we have Jesus, we already have the Lord's favor.

We may know that grace is a free gift, but resting in that reality does not come naturally to us. We can struggle with this concept of rest from our labors. We may feel condemnation if we aren't reading our Bibles daily. We may feel guilty taking a vacation because that means we must miss church. We may serve a meal to a member of the church who is ill because we feel pressure to work for God's favor or to please people or simply to check off that "service box" rather than because of the joy of it and love of neighbor. All the while Jesus lovingly and gently tells us, "Come to me, all who labor and are heavy laden, and I will give you rest" (Matthew 11:28).

Jesus says that his yoke is easy and his burden is light. By learning from him and taking up his yoke, we find rest for our souls (see Matthew 11:29–30). We can rest knowing that Jesus fulfilled all the law, that he died absorbing all our disobedience, all our worrying, all our vain attempts at working hard for our glory. He wants us to be free from the slavery of sin and free from the oppression of working for our salvation. His burden truly is light.

The Pharisees laid burdens on the people, outlining in complex detail all the rules they had to follow to live in line with the Law. The Pharisees didn't understand the concept of resting in God's grace.

In Matthew 12 we see that Jesus's disciples were criticized and challenged by the Pharisees for plucking heads of grain to eat on the Sabbath (see verses 1–2). Jesus reminded them of the time David, whom they revered as a hero of the faith, entered the tabernacle and ate the bread of the Presence, which was reserved for priests. He also mentioned that the priests worked on the Sabbath in violation of the commandment to rest. But God declared neither David nor the priests guilty (see verses 3–5). Jesus went on to explain that he is Lord of the Sabbath and his desire is for all to rest in him. He was not saying the Sabbath rest isn't necessary or important but that practicing the Sabbath is pointless when we focus on the duty rather than the gift. God desires mercy and not spiritual sacrifices (see verses 7–8).

Jesus kept working his miracles and healing on the Sabbath. The Pharisees still didn't get it and, as a result, conspired to kill him (see verses 9–14).

There are pharisaical tendencies in all of us. Jesus offers a better way—spiritual rest. He wants us to cast our burdens onto him. He wants us to learn to trust him and rest in him. This is how we rest well. Ultimately, we cannot rest in any way without this spiritual rest. We won't take every thought captive and submit it to the Lord until we understand that he will carry our burden. We won't stop running the race in our own strength until we believe we have a God who is stronger and able and willing to carry our load.

It's the spiritual rest that frees you and me from guilt. It's the spiritual rest that allows us to enjoy rest.

MAKING TIME FOR REST

To avoid repeating the error of the Pharisees, we must be careful not to prescribe a set of rules about what it looks like to fulfill the

Sabbath command. In other words, as you consider the following suggestions, be aware that they are only suggestions. The moment you begin to feel condemned for not meeting your Sabbath rest goals is the moment you've turned your rest into work. We want to enter into our day of rest acknowledging that it's ultimately a rest in Jesus—trusting him for our salvation and receiving his amazing grace.

One suggestion for carving out time for rest is to schedule it as you'd schedule work and other commitments. Because of my line of work, I must be extremely intentional about when I rest; otherwise I could work *all* the time. For me, a day without deliberately scheduled periods of rest might look like this: wake up and check e-mail, send e-mails, get kids off to school, write an article, attend a meeting, write another article, check my phone (every other minute), clean the kitchen, pick up the kids, cook dinner, check my e-mail, put kids to bed, write an article, answer e-mails, check phone one last time before bed.

I wish I could say this scenario has never happened, but it describes my days more accurately than I'd like to admit. I must schedule breaks; otherwise I'll keep working. So I try to schedule some time every day for Bible reading. I also try to get out and walk, run, or cycle for a certain portion of each day. And I try to designate one full day each week to rest, which for me typically involves church, fellowship with friends, exercise, and time with family. When I've worked hard throughout the week, it frees me to rest well, guilt free.

Reading the Bible and praying aren't our only means of entering into Sabbath rest, but I've personally found them to be important and essential elements. It's hard for me to rest in Jesus when I'm not reminding myself of the truth of his Word. I find it restful to remind myself that it is only by grace that I am saved and not by works. I can rest in Jesus knowing it depends not one bit on anything I do. Oh, what joy! What peace! That's the rest we need most of all.

THE BENEFITS OF PLAY

Recently, my dear friend Amy and I were reminiscing about the good ol' days. You know, those days of reckless abandonment and little to no responsibility. We weren't actually reckless, but we were young and fancy-free. During college we'd often go out late and stay up talking deep into the night or even into the early morning hours. I remember bringing home Thai food at ten o'clock at night and giggling until about three in the morning. (I know. Wild and crazy, right?) Beyond discussing which boy liked which girl, praying for friends and for our own decisions about the future, keeping one another spiritually accountable, and dreaming about what we were going to do the next semester, we simply didn't have much that was burdening us.

But in the years that followed, we encountered marriages and miscarriages, cancer and death, friends committing adultery and friends falling away from the faith. Add in mortgages and endless laundry, babies and debt, and the ever-increasing need to pray for strong marriages as we watched couples falling apart around us. Today my conversations with Amy are no less enjoyable than in our younger years, but they sound quite different. One time we both realized how weighty our discussions had become and wondered if the world had changed that much or if it'd always been like this and we were just more aware of it.

The older I get, the harder I have to fight to keep a sense of wonder in everyday life. By contrast, when my daughter wakes up, besides being quite concerned about her outfit for the day, she's generally carefree. Every moment is playtime.

Have you ever watched children play? They don't ever seem to get bored with doing the same thing over and over again. My daughter begs to go to the same park that we've visited hundreds of times, and she will sit in the sand pit for hours. Grab the bucket, put sand in it, dump the bucket out. Repeat. Over and over again. As adults, it's burdensome to even think about sand and kids. Will they ever get it out of their hair? Will I ever get the sand out of the carpet? Their bed will feel like it has little granules of sand in it *forever*. You know what I mean! Kids are content and free to play. We are concerned and worried.

In an essay on the Christian and play, Erik Thoennes, a professor of theology and biblical studies, wrote:

> Play is not a major emphasis in the Bible, and it can be unhelpful to encourage play in a culture that so often and easily trivializes God and life itself. Yet I do believe that a sense of play is necessary for a healthy Christian perspective on life. The failure to appreciate play in the Christian life could easily turn piety into sanctimony, reverence into rigidity, and sanctification into stuffiness. We must take God as seriously as we can, but never ourselves.[4]

I wholeheartedly agree—we must take God seriously but never ourselves. This concept and quote could easily sum up the entire point of this book. We must not take ourselves so seriously that we forget the wonder, we forget to delight, we forget the joy of living, and most important, we forget the God who gives it all to us.

What would happen if we learned to play well?

What a delight it is to go out with my kids on a rainy day and splash around! I wouldn't have thought twice about doing that as a child. It's a joy and my kids have a blast. You and I can't go around naively behaving as if there weren't evil in the world that we should pray about and be rightly concerned with. But despite that reality, we have so many reasons to rejoice and enjoy life to the full.

In his essay, Thoennes gave five reasons to understand and appreciate play, two of which I found especially helpful. First, he said that "play is a unique, God-given, universal, human experience."[5] What most fascinates me about this point is that play is indeed universal. A smile is a smile in St. Louis, Missouri, as much as it is a smile in Phnom Penh, Cambodia. Laughter is just as contagious in Aurora, Colorado, as it is in Yaoundé, Cameroon. God is so good to allow his created people to play and laugh and enjoy. Play is a beautiful reflection of the good and gracious and joyous nature of our God. What joy God must have experienced as he created the world. Think of the long-necked giraffe and the massive whale that blows water out of a hole in its back, or the intricately designed ladybug and creative diversity among the butterflies. Can you imagine God having fun as he designed them? I think if we realize that we are God's image bearers and reflect aspects of his character, then, yes, we can.

Second, Thoennes suggested that "play tends to be seen as either frivolous or an end in itself." He said,

> Play, especially within sport, tends to be dismissed as
> meaningless, worldly, and contrary to sober Christian
> living. On the other hand, Christians can be pulled into

the idolatry of sport and leisure as an end in itself to be
sought at all costs. A biblical understanding of play as
given by God for his glory and our good, but never an end
itself, will help coaches, athletes, and soccer moms
appreciate play and use it as a conduit of glorifying God.
Such a re-orientation will give perspective to our lives as
intended. "So, whether you eat or drink, or whatever you
do, do all to the glory of God" (1 Corinthians 10:31).[6]

Amen! You and I can rest to the glory of God. We can play to
the glory of God. When it's not about us, there's such freedom to
enjoy it. Play is a gift from the Lord. Whether we eat or drink,
splash in puddles of water or listen to music, ride our bikes or run
on a trail, play a game of Ultimate Frisbee or Monopoly, whatever
we do, we can do it all to the glory of God. So by all means, let's
do it!

THE WELL-RESTED SOUL

It's not often you'll have a friend tell you, *Hey, you, stop what you
are doing right now and go play or read or sleep or do whatever it
is that you find restful.* This is me telling you to do this! It will
transform your life. Besides enjoying God, which we'll explore
later in the book, I'm not sure if there's any more important concept for us to grapple with when it comes to enjoying the gifts of
God. If we don't learn to rest well, we'll worry ourselves to the
grave. Families will be neglected, tensions will run high, and we
will be left rundown and weary if we don't get this. So let's learn
to unplug, say no, and sit—or dance!

Here's God's Word to us who are desperately in need of rest:

He does not faint or grow weary; his understanding is
unsearchable. He gives power to the faint, and to him who
has no might he increases strength. Even youths shall faint
and be weary, and young men shall fall exhausted; but
they who wait for the LORD shall renew their strength;
they shall mount up with wings like eagles; they shall run
and not be weary; they shall walk and not faint. (Isaiah
40:28–31)

God is always working, and he is always working for our
good. He doesn't grow weary and tired, and he doesn't grow weary
and tired of *our* weariness. He will give us the power we need to
rest and play well. The Lord renews the strength of his people.
You can rest in him knowing that he's already done the heavy lift-
ing of your greatest need—salvation—and now he invites you to
receive that gift and rest in your soul.

Ultimately, the only way to fully enjoy the gift of rest is to
remember that your true rest is in Jesus—he is your Sabbath rest.
I'm so thankful our God doesn't require us to come to him put
together and strong. Instead he says we can come to him rundown
in our souls, we can come to him weary of trying so hard to do the
right thing, we can come to him flat on our faces, tired of running
the fight of faith, and he will not condemn us. Instead he will give
us rest. He is truly awesome.

Rejoice in what Jesus has already done for you, and then embrace the gift he's given to you: the freedom and joy of rest.

Not long ago my family embarked on an adventure of

building sandcastles and catching waves. We took off for the white sandy beaches of the Gulf Coast. Few activities thrill me more than watching my kids play, and I was eager to jump in there and play with them. I looked forward to days of relaxing without having to answer calls or e-mails. I could wake up late, go to bed whenever I desired, and spend time reading my Bible with the sounds of ocean waves in the background.

Of course, things didn't go exactly as expected. The trip south to the coast was a blast, and when we got to the beach, my youngest couldn't wait to see it. We all ran onto the beach and quickly realized that going to the beach in March is quite different from going to the beach in July. It was nippy, to say the least.

The next day, with the sun shining brightly, my husband headed to work and I headed to the beach with the kids. The Gulf Coast winds were chilly even with the sun out, and it was still too cold for me to get in the water—but not for my kids! So I sat on the beach, praying that the temperatures would miraculously rise. I didn't have a book with me. I had my phone, but it was only to capture this moment, not to scroll through e-mails and social media. I watched my children play in the water and sand. I helped them build a few castles, which I learned I'm pretty horrible at. Mostly I sat and delighted in soaking up all the beauty of the ocean and my children at play. It took work to sink into this quiet moment of rest and relaxation, partly because I was cold and partly because I'm not used to doing nothing. But I chose to thank the Lord for the opportunity to practice the joy of resting.

The Enjoy Project:
The Freedom to Press Pause

1. What hinders you from taking a Sabbath? Write down some ways you might adjust your habits or schedule to clear the way for a day of rest.

2. List some specific activities that help you rest, such as turning off your phone at night or listening to music, and others that prevent you from resting well.

3. Identify what you consider work. Then decide on a day to take entirely off from work, a day in which you will not do anything that you'd consider to be work, work related, or a distraction from rest. If your current commitments prevent you from taking a full day off, take as many hours for rest and relaxation as possible within a twenty-four-hour period. Write down what you learned, how you felt during and afterward, and what you struggled with.

4. What are some activities you consider to be play? Do as many of those activities as you can during this week's Enjoy Project, without neglecting your necessary work and responsibilities. Have fun to the glory of God! Reflect on your time of play. What difference did it make to be intentional in this area?

5. Evaluate your schedule. Do you have margins? Did you find it difficult to find time to rest and relax this week? If so, identify areas where you

can adjust your schedule to create space for
play.
6. Look back over the chapter to identify one idea
   or truth that really stands out. Find a way to put
   that into practice this week.
7. Sabbath rest is not only rest from work; it's also
   resting in the gospel. Pray and preach the
   gospel to yourself.

*What a gift you gave, Lord, when you
created humanity to enjoy play and to need
rest. In a broken world that feels so heavy,
you graciously made me in such a way that
play refreshes my heart. And far from being a
curse, the need to rest reminds me that I
don't have to do it all. Which is good, because I can't. Help me to know that I don't
have to keep on endlessly striving; I can trust
you enough to rest.*

Most people are

afraid to rest.

We're **afraid** to rest

because we don't

trust God

and instead

trust ourselves

to hold the world together.

—Justin Buzzard

Money, Possessions, and Joy

I remember one of the first nights as a child that my family needed to pack up and stay with our grandmother. My father worked hard but didn't always earn enough to cover the costs associated with feeding four girls and caring for his wife, so from time to time our electricity would be shut off. That's just what happens when you fall behind on your electricity bill. I was never upset with my parents; I knew they were trying as hard as they could. They wanted nothing but the best for us girls, so I just thought this was a part of life.

Those experiences when I was young taught me some lessons about money. First, I realized that it is fleeting and the pursuit of it for security is foolish. I knew that money would not go with me to the grave. Proverbs 23:5 captures this sentiment, though I had no understanding of this biblical truth at the time: "Cast but a glance at riches, and they are gone, for they will surely sprout wings and fly off to the sky like an eagle" (NIV). My father passed away when I was nineteen, without a cent to his name. But what my dad did leave was love—and lots of it. My father was generous with what he had. So I learned to give freely rather than cling to things that don't last beyond this world. What might be viewed as financial difficulties actually taught me to live free from the power of money.

But along with that positive lesson came an unhealthy comfort with ignoring the need to learn how to manage money. When I needed to go to college, I took out loans even though I had scholarships. I worked throughout college except for when I studied abroad for one semester and then took an internship in New York the second semester. That year I lived off debt. Although I realize that in some situations debt may be unavoidable, in my case I was simply foolish and didn't really understand what I was doing. I'd never been taught how to properly handle money or how to value the opportunities afforded me.

Many of us have a complicated relationship with money. Either we tend to worship it or, like me in early adulthood, we handle it foolishly. Either we are tempted to hoard it selfishly in fear of not having enough for ourselves, or we're inclined to blow it by living lavishly and beyond our means.

The Bible has much to say about money. In fact, author Randy Alcorn noted that Jesus taught more on the topic of money than he did on heaven and hell combined.[1] Clearly this topic is important to the Lord and therefore needs to be important to us. Since we can't cover everything the Bible says about money, I'd like to focus on two main aspects: (1) the challenge to show generosity to our neighbor, and (2) warnings against finding our treasure in riches. I'm convinced that learning and growing in these two ways can actually transform how we enjoy money and possessions.

GOD'S DESIGN FOR GENEROUS LIVING

I love how the Bible doesn't simply give us a list of rules—that's not its primary purpose. It points us to the truth of what matters most to God, and along the way we get glimpses into the lives of individuals who tried and sometimes struggled to follow God. This is particularly true of the passages that describe the early church. We get to witness how they wrestled their way to a deeper understanding of God and how to follow Jesus. And in 2 Corinthians 8 we get a lesson on generosity from the example of the churches in Macedonia.

You don't typically begin reading from the bottom up, right? You read from the top of the page and make your way to the bottom. But for this topic, I think it's important to start at the bottom of this section of Scripture. As Paul encouraged the Corinthians to be generous, he didn't do so by laying a guilt trip on them, nor did he *command* them to give. In fact, he said, "I say this not as a command, but to prove by the earnestness of others that your love also is genuine" (verse 8).

Paul then pointed to Jesus as an example of humility and the ultimate example of giving: "For you know the grace of our Lord Jesus Christ, that though he was rich, yet for your sake he became poor, so that you by his poverty might become rich" (verse 9). There is no greater example of this than the fact that Jesus, who was the Word and was with God, and was God (see John 1:1–3), put on flesh, was born into a poor family, and lived among us. The mere fact that he put on flesh is astonishing in and of itself. Jesus became nothing so that we could gain everything. We love because he first loved us. We give because of the joy of emulating our Savior.

Like every other good thing, material blessings are a gift from God, meant to be enjoyed as a reminder of his character and a reflection of it. Wealth is not intended to be a goal in itself, nor is it something to be feared. As Alcorn noted,

> God comes right out and tells us why He gives us more money than we need. It's not so we can find more ways to spend it. It's not so we can indulge ourselves and spoil our children. It's not so we can insulate ourselves from needing God's provision.
>
> It's so we can *give*—generously.[2]

I think it's important to establish that generosity, true and pure generosity, never comes from obligation or force. Paul wrapped it up well in 2 Corinthians 9:6–7: "The point is this: whoever sows sparingly will also reap sparingly, and whoever sows bountifully will also reap bountifully. Each one must give as he has decided in his heart, not reluctantly or under compulsion, for God loves a cheerful giver." And this is exactly what the churches in Macedonia were doing. They were suffering great poverty yet they still gave, not reluctantly but out of an abundance of joy (see 8:1–2). Some gave according to their means, while others gave beyond their means. What I love about this account is that Paul notes that the people begged to take part in the relief of the saints (see 8:4).

I understand this feeling the Macedonians must have experienced. Gift giving could be classified as one of my love languages. I love to give gifts, think about gifts, imagine the look on the recipient's face, and think of creative things to give. At times I've even begged my husband, in particular, to let me do something for him. I have such fun. I *enjoy* giving, and out of an abundance of joy, I want to give.

The Macedonians also gave themselves, first to the Lord and then to their brothers (see 8:5). They weren't only giving financially; they were eager to offer any other help. Giving isn't solely about money and material things. And this is where I break from the Macedonians. I love giving gifts, but it's tough for me to give my time. I'm selfish and must fight against anxiety when I need to adjust what I'm doing or change my plans for someone else. I want to be like the Macedonians, eager and excited to give beyond material and monetary gifts.

These Macedonians weren't rich, but this wasn't about riches. It was about their hearts. They were giving whatever they had, cheerfully. It's the same for you and me. We can give abundantly out of a feeling of obligation, but that isn't what the Lord is after. He doesn't need your money; he desires your heart. He wants to transform you into a cheerful giver. He desires you and me to be women who love to give and serve. He wants generosity to flow out of the abundance of joy in our hearts.

If you've found giving to be difficult, Paul has gospel encouragement for you: "God is able to make all grace abound to you, so that having all sufficiency in all things at all times, you may abound in every good work" (2 Corinthians 9:8). God gives the grace that enables us to give joyfully and causes us to abound in every good work. Generosity is his work in us, and we can be sure that if you and I ask God to give us hearts that give cheerfully, he who is faithful will surely do it.

GIVING THROUGH HOSPITALITY

As I mentioned earlier, our giving doesn't necessarily have to be financial or material. We can make a great impact, for example, by giving our time, specifically in the area of hospitality. Most of us, even with little, can open up our spaces for others. But we often find ourselves avoiding any opportunity to welcome others, due to inadequate space or messy homes.

I love to host people in my home—the more the merrier! The idea of one day owning a bed-and-breakfast and preparing eggs, bacon, grits, biscuits, gravy—all the southern fixin's you can imagine—for strangers who have traveled far and wide makes this Tennessee girl jump for joy! Hospitality is not a burden to me, usually. But a recent move from a ranch-style home with three bedrooms and a full basement to a two-bedroom apartment has left me with far less space for hosting. The apartment is spacious enough but definitely smaller.

When we first moved across the state to this new area, I hesitated to say that I lived in an apartment. When people asked where I lived, I'd say something like, "I live in the neighborhood off the interstate." It wasn't long before the Lord convicted me of pride and fear of man. Worldliness and covetousness had crept into my heart. Thank you, Lord, for that revelation and the repentance that followed!

Soon after our move, visiting friends began to request to stay in our apartment. There's a temptation to wait until everything is "perfect"—as in having a large, clean, beautiful home—before allowing someone in. To me, our new home felt too small to truly be welcoming. And because of the lack of space, boxes were still piled up in public spaces. For a while I felt as if we lived in a box filled with boxes. Did I mention that we have two children? So it was a box filled with boxes *and* toys. *There's no way I can invite people over,* I thought. But over the past few years, the Lord has been teaching me about the meaning of serving and giving to others and about the meaning of true hospitality—what it is and what it is not. I've been reminded that hospitality is a matter of the heart, not square footage or neatness.

Hospitality Is About Love

The apostle Peter urged his readers to "show hospitality to one another without grumbling" (1 Peter 4:9). Hospitality was a commonly expected practice in the first century. So Peter reminded Christians not to complain about this common activity. Surrounding his call to hospitality, Peter told believers to "keep loving one another earnestly" and "as each has received a gift, use it to serve one another" (verses 8, 10).

Hospitality is an easy way to bless others with the gifts you've been blessed with. It is a practical way to love your neighbor as yourself.

Hospitality Is About the Heart

It is possible to invite guests into a completely clean home with every room in order, plenty of space, and a prepared meal that a five-star restaurant would envy and yet not be hospitable. Too often we run around like Martha, "distracted with much serving" rather than sitting and enjoying our guests as Mary did when she sat at Jesus's feet (see Luke 10:38–42).

Love transforms hospitality. When you begin to think about serving others and sharing not only your space but also your heart, you can open the doors with gladness. Paul charged the early

Christians to "contribute to the needs of the saints and seek to show hospitality" (Romans 12:13). Hospitality and caring for the needs of others is a mark of our faith. Nowhere did Paul qualify his command. He did not say, "Show hospitality but only if you have a lot of room and all your possessions are neatly stored." Don't wait until everything seems perfect; offer what you have out of love, and trust God to bless your guests. This mirrors the call of the Macedonians in many ways. They didn't wait to give after obtaining earthly riches; otherwise they might never have given.

By the grace of God, I did not hesitate for long before we invited guests into our new home. In fact, we've seen more feet travel through our 1,200-square-foot living space than we ever did in our house in the same short period of time.

It's good to remember that hospitality isn't about the what, when, and where. It's about the who and the why. Hospitality is about the person we get to welcome in and love. We can trust that the Lord will bless those who come into our doors if we have hearts to serve and love them. Your guests might not remember your space, but they will surely remember your care. Opening our homes may seem like a major undertaking, but we can do it with joy when we view it as an expression of thanks to the Lord, who gave everything to live among us and die on the cross in our place.

GETTING A PROPER PERSPECTIVE
ON POSSESSIONS

In Mark 10:17–22 we read the story of a rich young man, a story that begins with great hope and ends in deep sorrow.

Jesus was on his way to Jerusalem when a rich young man ran to him and knelt. The young man knew Jesus was important. He also knew the Law. What he didn't know, we come to find out, is the depths of his own heart.

The young ruler called Jesus "Good Teacher," and although that indeed is true, Jesus deflected this title and told him that only the Father is good. Jesus, I believe, was doing two things in the next few verses. First, he was making sure the man understood that Jesus is God—if only God is good, and Jesus is good, then Jesus must also be God. Second, he began to establish that the rich young ruler, who thought he was good, was not so good after all. If we believe we are good, we won't see our desperate need for saving grace.

Jesus listed the commandments, and the young man acknowledged that he had obeyed them all from the time he was a child. The rich young ruler thought he was doing great. Of course, we know he couldn't have obeyed them all as perfectly as he said, but Jesus, who is all-knowing and all-loving, directed the attention not on whether the young man's answer was accurate but on what was happening in his heart. He knew the idol beneath the surface. Jesus wasn't trying to play "gotcha!" Instead, "Jesus, looking at him, loved him, and said to him, 'You lack one thing: go, sell all that you have and give to the poor, and you will have treasure in heaven; and come, follow me'" (verse 21). Oh, what love! That Jesus would identify the one thing the young ruler lacked so that he might gain *all* things in him (see 2 Peter 1:3).

But we know the unfortunate end to the story. The rich young ruler went away sorrowful. His possessions were too great—not so much in their material worth but to the extent they controlled his heart. He couldn't imagine life without all his stuff, even if that life meant he had Jesus. After he walked away, Jesus used the opportunity to share a lesson with the disciples who had witnessed the interaction. It's hard, he said, for people with lots of stuff to enter the kingdom of God. Astonished, the disciples asked, "Then who can be saved?" Jesus reassured them that God can do the impossible in the hearts of men (Mark 10:26–27).

Do you identify with the rich young ruler? Perhaps you find peace and security in stuff, whether that means having designer appliances, the newest tech device, or a luxurious vacation. Too often, the tangible, visible things of our lives become the pillars that uphold our peace. And any time these things are shaken—when a sickness sets in, our best friend is unavailable, or a hailstorm wrecks the roof—our pillars start to crumble and our peace collapses. When we, like the rich young ruler, look to stuff and to riches for security and satisfaction, the Bible calls this idolatry. Anything, even good things, that we value more than God is an idol. Anything other than God on which we rest our current peace and future hope is an idol.

So where's your hope? If Jesus said to drop it all and follow him, would you be able to do it? Would you be willing to open your home for someone to live in, perhaps, or to give sacrificially to your church or an organization—and do it with joy? These are the tough questions we must ask ourselves, especially in regard to wealth. In Matthew's account of the rich young man, he recorded Jesus warning his disciples, "Truly, I say to you, only with difficulty will a rich person enter the kingdom of heaven" (19:23). Wealth can blind us. We begin to believe we are self-sufficient and no longer need God. The pursuit of wealth can draw our hearts into dangerous and dark places. It becomes our trap instead of our joy.

Some of us stumble into a different trap when it comes to our view of material things. We can view all wealth as evil and judge those who have more than us. Or we assume we must literally give it all away or we aren't truly sacrificing. A friend once lamented to me about living in a home with running water and electricity. She felt selfish. She was carrying a burden of sacrifice that the Lord never asked her to bear. We read in the Old Testament that God gave riches (see 1 Kings 3:11–13; 2 Chronicles 9:22). And we know from the New Testament that every good thing comes from the Father (see James 1:17). God gives and he takes away—but we also know that he never does anything against his character. If God promised to give Solomon riches, for example, those riches could not have been sinful in and of themselves. It would be against God's nature since God is pure and righteous. So the issue isn't wealth but the condition of our hearts.

To be clear, I am not speaking of receiving a blessing from the Lord because of good works. In other words, the unbiblical prosperity gospel would argue that if you obey God, you will receive wealth, health, and prosperity. That is not true. God does as he wills, and our obedience does not earn God's favor. We can know, however, that if we have received wealth in an honorable manner (for example, if we haven't stolen money, lied or cheated to get ahead, or cheated on our taxes), then our wealth can be used to glorify God, and we can rest in our hearts. Therefore, we can indeed take joy in how a new set of curtains brightens up the kitchen if it points us to gratitude and not to entitlement or greed.

Like greed, guilt hinders us from fully enjoying our money and possessions. We miss out on God's intent when we equate any wealth with sin. Riches aren't a sin. It's the heart that causes the sin. To guard against feelings of guilt, ask God to help you to steward your blessings well.

Fear can also keep us from enjoying God's gifts, propelling comparison and shame. You can be ashamed of your small home or out-of-style furnishings. You can be ashamed of your inability to give. But as we've seen, what's important is not a matter of wealth but giving out of the abundance of joy. Again, it's about the heart.

The mouth speaks what the heart feels (see Luke 6:45). When we feel guilty or fearful, it can lead to complaining. When we are discontent or struggle with envy, we might assume the worst of others who have more. We judge others and assume they are greedy and selfish. If you constantly hunger for others' possessions, you will not be satisfied with what you have. And frankly, you will never be satisfied unless you are satisfied with and in Christ. Nothing on this earth can truly fulfill what you need.

Ultimately, as we fight to enjoy the gift of our money and possessions, we fight to keep the end in mind. This is not our final resting place. We don't want to get to the end of life and, like the Preacher in Ecclesiastes, lament, "Then I considered all that my hands had done and the toil I had expended in doing it, and behold, all was vanity and a striving after wind, and there was nothing to be gained under the sun" (2:11).

Let's not chase after the wind.

Do you believe God will provide for you in deeper ways than by providing things? And do you know and believe that giving should come out of a cheerful, generous, and free heart? Do you enjoy watching to see how he will provide and who he will bless through you?

You may have answered no. Maybe you *want* to say yes. Maybe you *want* to believe, but you are honest enough with your heart to know you're not there. If so, be encouraged. Jesus calls you to radically follow him, but it's not by your own strength. Remember what he told the disciples: what's impossible for man is possible with God (see Mark 10:27). It's impossible for you to change yourself. But God promises to finish the good work he began in you (see Philippians 1:6). If you discover that your faith is placed in your wealth and your possessions, ask God to help you find your security in him. His promises are true. In him, you are secure.

A CHANGE OF HEART

The grass is always greener on the other side, isn't it? We long for things—good things—but so often it seems God has a different lesson for us as we wait. Sometimes it takes a wake-up call from our loving Savior to help us see how we are not enjoying his good gifts to us.

My friend Gena shared with me how she experienced such a wake-up call. It all started with her desire for a house she and her family could call their own.

"We were renters," she explained, "and I just hated not being able to have the perceived freedom of owning my own home. We couldn't paint the walls or change the flooring. There were limitations on what kinds of pets we could have and how many visitors could stay with us at one time." Gena envisioned a house with a yard for her children to play in, maybe even one with a swimming pool and a rose garden, like her grandmother's home. "I had dreams about having friends over for dinner parties and holiday barbeques," she continued. "Maybe even putting on a Christmas play with the neighborhood kids." In anticipation of "someday," she spent time thumbing through magazines to clip out color schemes and decorating ideas.

Wrapped up in her longing for this dream house, she became

discontent with their rental home. "I could find a hundred excuses as to why it wasn't working for us," she said. "In retrospect, I can now appreciate our quiet neighborhood, amazing neighbors, and the little bit of yard space where we would have impromptu picnics on nice afternoons." But caught up in finding a way to make her dream a reality, she convinced her husband to downgrade to an apartment. "My thought process was that it would be less comfortable, and thus more of a motivation to save the money for a house," she confessed. "It would also save us money each month that we could put toward a down payment on a house."

Discontent followed her to the new apartment, and she complained regularly to her husband about feeling cramped in the smaller space, crowded by the neighbors, and limited in her ability to entertain guests. "I was also trying to negotiate with God, suggesting that if he would bless us with a home, *then* I would open my home for Bible studies and fellowship." She admitted she even stopped taking care of the apartment properly. "I think I was hoping my husband would see that as evidence that we needed more space and would move faster on purchasing a house."

One day the Lord spoke to Gena's heart, bringing to mind Luke 16:10: "Whoever can be trusted with very little can also be trusted with much, and whoever is dishonest with very little will also be dishonest with much" (NIV). She was immediately convicted about her attitude and behavior. "I was not trustworthy with our little apartment. I didn't care for it or appreciate the blessing that it was. I wasn't grateful for a roof over my head, indoor plumbing, hot water, and a safe place for my family to live. I took for granted the hard work my husband endured every day to provide for us. I wasn't grateful. I wasn't a good steward. I was oblivious to the blessings that God had given our family."

Gena prayed for a change of attitude. And she took steps to enjoy the home she already had. "I began to organize the apartment, adding special touches to create a feeling of home. I started hosting play dates with other moms from our church." In doing so, she learned to recognize the blessings of their apartment. "I found contentment. I didn't need a change of housing. I needed a change of heart."

Two years later the family purchased their first house. It doesn't look anything like the one she'd hoped for all those years, but she told me, "It is entirely perfect."

As Gena learned, choosing contentment allows us to see and enjoy the gifts from God that are right in front of us.

ETERNAL TREASURES

One of the first and probably hardest ways for us to enjoy God's gift of material blessings is by giving them away. Giving is a touchy subject. Preachers, I've heard, either love challenging congregations to give or avoid the subject for fear of offending everyone in the room. But if we have a biblical understanding of giving and God's material gifts, then we see that we are never to be compelled and generosity is to always come from our own conviction and through a cheerful heart. We may need to ask God to soften our hearts and move us toward generosity, including with our tithing.

When we give, and that includes giving to the church, we want to give out of an abundance of joy. God loves a cheerful giver, so ask him to change your heart and give you a biblical perspective on giving. As we seek the Lord in this area, he will be faithful and we will undoubtedly begin to enjoy giving.

At the end of the day, we must look toward eternity for all our satisfaction. Earthly treasures are all but a breath away from being gone, but we have a treasure that will never rot or be destroyed (see Matthew 6:19–20). Our deepest and greatest treasure must be Christ. "For the things that are seen are transient, but the things that are unseen are eternal" (2 Corinthians 4:18). We are indeed living in the already and not yet. Let us treasure Christ above all else and look to that forever, eternal treasure.

Having eternity in mind helps us to keep our eyes on the prize. Heaven is our home. We want to store up treasures in heaven because those are the only treasures that will last (see Matthew 6:20–21). We want to resist the temptation to give *only* because we will be rewarded, but let's not forget the awesome truth that a prize awaits you and me in heaven (see Philippians 3:14).

Finally, let's go out and actually enjoy our God-given money and possessions. We can do so in any number of ways. We can take a vacation, purchase a sweater, buy a bike. We can donate to a nonprofit organization, sponsor a child, or give a meal to the homeless man on the corner. We can use our money to serve others through hospitality. The list is endless, and so many of our opportunities to enjoy can and will be others focused. If it is all God's, we should be able to freely enjoy what he has given us. Vacations, recreation, vehicles, homes, and more can be enjoyed guilt free when we view them as gifts from the Lord.

The Enjoy Project:
Money, Possessions, and Joy

1. What most often hinders you from the enjoyment of possessions and money? What are some ways you can begin to fight against guilt, fear, envy, complaining, or forgetting your true home?

2. Think about some of the possessions God has given you that you enjoy deeply. Find a way to share in the enjoyment of those possessions with someone else this week.

3. What is one area where you could increase your giving? Think of how you might implement a plan of action to begin stewarding your funds so that giving becomes more natural and joyful.

4. Give. Find a way to give this week. Ask the Lord for opportunities, whether financially or through the gifts of hospitality or your time.

5. Identify one method of giving that might not come naturally for you. For example, maybe it's harder for you to give time than money. Be intentional this week about giving in that way and reflect on that experience.

6. Look back over the chapter to identify one idea or truth that really stands out. Find a way to put that into practice this week.

7. Remember that you want to give of your own accord. Don't give out of guilt, fear, or a sense of obligation. Ask the Lord to give you a heart

that gives cheerfully. Pray and preach the gospel to yourself.

Lord, help me to remember that all I have comes from you. And your call to me is to live generously, stewarding what you have entrusted to me. Keep me from idolizing and finding my identity in the things I have. As one who is found in Christ, thank you that my identity has been graciously and unshakably established. Free me from desperately clinging to the things of this world and help me to hold fast to you.

If more of us valued

food and *cheer*

and song

above hoarded gold,

it would be a

merrier world.

—J. R. R. Tolkien

Taste and See

I shared in the last chapter that the thought of owning a little bed-and-breakfast excites me. I do enjoy guests and hosting, but what makes my imagination go wild is daydreaming about the various recipes I'd have the opportunity to create. Would I change the menu every day? Perhaps I'd serve an English style breakfast with eggs, bacon, scones, sausage, freshly whipped butter, and jam. My mouth is watering as I ponder these things!

But it's not only the idea of having a bed-and-breakfast that gets me excited about food. Recently I bought a cookbook with recipes from Jerusalem and cooked through the book for my family. Another time I bought a cookbook filled with Star Wars–inspired goodies and cooked the recipes with my son. It was such fun. When I eat out, depending on where we go, I try to identify the spices in my meal, just in case I can re-create it—because *I love food.*

I love food as a means of sustenance, but mostly I love the taste of a variety of foods. I enjoy the opportunity food affords us to host, and I love that food brings my family together at least once a day and often twice. We don't miss dinner together unless one of us is traveling, and we enjoy family breakfasts as often as we can.

ROOM AT THE TABLE

Food played an important role in the first-century church as an opportunity for Christians to gather and fellowship. Most sojourners and travelers could not afford lodging houses and so would depend on the generosity of others for shelter.[1] As a matter of fact, welcoming strangers and others into one's home was such a central and important aspect of the Greco-Roman culture that being hospitable is listed as a qualification for those seeking to oversee a church (see 1 Timothy 3:2; Titus 1:7–8).

Perhaps this is why we are challenged by the New Testament writers to show love to our neighbor through hospitality (see Romans 12:13; 1 Peter 4:8–9). If a major part of hospitality includes food, could we conclude that sharing food is also a way of showing love to our neighbor and our fellow believers? I think so. As we'll see in the paragraphs that follow, God invites us to a feast. It's one of the many ways he shows his love for us, so when we share with others, we mirror that love. But Peter noted we're to do it without grumbling. As we discovered so clearly in the last chapter, God desires us to give, but it must be with a cheerful heart. This means he cares about your attitude toward those with whom you share the table.

In the first-century church, attitudes toward food and with whom one would eat revealed the condition of an individual's heart. Peter struggled greatly with the fear of what others might think of him. He battled it as Jesus walked toward his death (see John 18:15–27), and he seemed to continue to stumble in this area from time to time. In Galatians 2:11–14, we get a picture of Peter's battle as it related to eating with those who were not like him. At times Peter would eat with Gentiles who did not observe Jewish food restrictions, but when certain men came around, he would withdraw himself from the Gentiles. Paul said Peter would separate himself, "fearing the circumcision party" (verse 12). Unfortunately, because Peter was a leader in the church, his hypocrisy prompted other Jews and even another leader, Barnabas, to withdraw from the Gentiles too (see verse 13).

The trouble here, besides that Peter and others who followed his example were simply unkind and hurtful, is that this withdrawal stood in opposition to the gospel. His refusal to eat with Gentiles signified that in order to have a place at his table, they would need to eat as he did, observing Jewish tradition and law rather than living in the freedom of grace.

Although we may not deny someone a seat at our table, we can be tempted similarly as we judge others who eat differently than we do. While the organic, sugar-free, gluten-free health trends definitely assist those who need to eat in certain ways, they can also, if we allow our hearts to judge, lead to isolation. It's not the food choices that isolate others necessarily but our judgmental language or secret unkind thoughts when others don't share our priorities. Conversely, we can harm our neighbor who truly has food allergies and aversions by dismissing their dietary needs as just a trend or a fad. Holding our opinions about food over others can cause unnecessary divisions in our relationships. Instead of serving as a means for connection and fellowship, food becomes a source of division, as it did for some people in the early church.

Paul was seriously concerned about these implications because they were "not in step with the truth of the gospel" (verse

14). He rebuked Peter, saying, "If you, though a Jew, live like a Gentile and not like a Jew, how can you force the Gentiles to live like Jews?" (verse 14). Paul then reminded Peter and the Jewish Christians that "we ourselves are Jews by birth and not Gentile sinners; yet we know that a person is not justified by works of the law but through faith in Jesus Christ" (verses 15–16). This scene alone gives you and me a picture of just how complex and important food was in the early church and can still be today. How one relates to food has gospel implications. We can't be saved by our traditions, and the table is an important place to not only display that reality but also to show the power of Jesus to unite all who believe in him.

Ultimately, food points us to Jesus. He uses it to display his goodness and glory. The enjoyment of food may seem trivial, but as we understand the beauty of how Jesus uses it to point to the gospel, food is transformed into another opportunity to enjoy God's creation.

THE BREAD OF LIFE

If you've had the joy of eating out at an American restaurant, you'll know that one of the first items brought to the table is often a basket of bread. And it's bottomless! You eat that basket of bread and—*voila!*—another basket filled with bread appears. Many of us fill up on bread before our main dish even has a chance to make its appearance! For centuries bread has been a staple in many diets around the world. Bread certainly was an essential part of the diet for people living in the era of the Old and New Testaments. One of the most famous stories in the Bible involves bread, and a lot of it.

Jesus was at the Sea of Tiberias. A large crowd followed him there because of the miracles he performed on the sick (see John 6:1–2). Jews were celebrating the Passover, but this crowd following Jesus apparently did not have food. Jesus saw the big crowds and asked one of his disciples, Philip, where he could buy bread so everyone could eat (see verse 5). Philip answered that two hundred denarii, the equivalent of approximately seven months of wages, wouldn't even be enough to buy bread for each person to have a little (see Matthew 20:2; John 6:7). Andrew, another disciple, pointed out that a young boy had five barley loaves and two fish (see John 6:8–9). You know the rest of this amazing story: Jesus turned those small portions into enough to feed five thousand.

What's amazing to me about the story isn't necessarily the miracle of Jesus feeding five thousand but the generosity in which he did so. Jesus was an incredible servant. He distributed the bread but didn't dictate how much each person could have. He gave them "as much as they wanted," and he didn't stop until they had "eaten their fill" (verses 11–12). Doesn't that remind you of the amazing grace of our God poured out abundantly for us? It's never ending. The crowd responded by declaring Jesus a prophet, probably thinking about the promise to Moses in Deuteronomy 18:15, "The LORD your God will raise up for you a prophet like me from among you, from your brothers—it is to him you shall listen," which was fulfilled in Jesus.

After this miracle Jesus withdrew from the crowd, walked on water, and crossed the sea to Capernaum. When the crowd realized he was no longer there, they sought to find him. Have you ever lost something and then went into a panicked search? I can't imagine what the crowd must have felt as they realized they had "lost" Jesus. That this miracle worker was no longer among them. They were frantic and even jumped into boats to search for him. Their searching and persistence was rewarded but maybe not how they would have expected.

When the crowd found him, Jesus immediately rebuked them for having wrong motives in their desire for him. In short, they wanted to find Jesus because their bellies were full and not because of what they had seen him do. They were seeking the gift rather than the Giver (see John 6:26). Jesus told them not to labor for food that perishes but for the food that endures to eternal life. And because he is awesome, Jesus told them he would also give that to them. He said, "For the bread of God is he who comes down from heaven and gives life to the world" (verse 33). He explained that *he* is the Bread of Life and "whoever comes to me shall not hunger, and whoever believes in me shall never thirst" (verse 35). The hunger and thirst are spiritual in nature. Those who believe and trust in him will never hunger or thirst spiritually. We are satisfied when we seek our satisfaction in God alone.

These verses are incredibly rich with promises for those who place their trust in Jesus, but his statements didn't sit well with many. They didn't get it. How could Jesus be manna from heaven? Again helping relate the importance of food back to spirituality, Jesus said, "Whoever feeds on my flesh and drinks my blood has eternal life, and I will raise him up on the last day" (verse 54). Jesus was not speaking literally here but looking ahead to the wonderful parallel to the Lord's Supper, where Christians break the bread and drink the wine as a metaphorical reminder of all Jesus has done for us through the gospel (see 1 Corinthians 11:23–32). Again, this is an incredible use of food as a way to remind us of our true and better satisfaction through Jesus.

"Whoever feeds on this bread will live forever" (John 6:58). Jesus will keep you and me forever. This bread is the ultimate bread—the feast we want to seek after. It's the Bread of Life—it's Jesus. No weight gain to be concerned about! We can't feast too much on this bread. Yes, there is denial involved, but it's not like denying apple pie to instead eat applesauce. It's like denying an orange that has begun to rot, with an outer shell gray from decay, for freshly squeezed orange juice from a citrus harvester. It's so much better in every way.

It's clear that food was an essential theme in the Scriptures for displaying the awesomeness of Christ. And one of our rewards for feasting on the True Bread now will be feasting in heaven on food like we would have found in Eden. Revelation describes that there will be much rejoicing when the bride of Christ, his church, joins him in heaven. It will be a party. "Blessed are those who are invited to the marriage supper of the Lamb" (Revelation 19:9). Isaiah prophesied about this great feast: "On this mountain the LORD of hosts will make for all peoples a feast of rich food, a feast of well-aged wine, of rich food full of marrow, of aged wine well refined" (25:6).

Can you imagine? Have you ever thought about how amazing the feast will be in heaven? One of the motivators for enjoying food today is that it's given by God as a gift we will delight in for eternity. Enjoying food is not trivial—it will be a central theme of our celebrating in heaven. Amazing!

As much as I've already written about food in the Bible, I feel like I've only scratched the surface. There's much in the Word about this gift and also about our struggle with it. But we don't have to read our Bibles to know we have a problem with food; all we must do is look at our hearts and habits to know there's trouble.

THE BITTER FRUIT OF THE FALL

As much as I enjoy food at times, I have a bit of a love/hate relationship with it as well. Over the past ten years I've suffered from a severe form of GERD (gastroesophageal reflux disease). It all stemmed from an allergic reaction to antibiotics that resulted in thrush, which strips good and bad bacteria from your digestive system. My stomach has suffered ever since. This means I must watch what I eat, and during flare-ups I must abstain from things like cake, ice cream, tomato sauces, chocolate, pasta, bread, cheese, coffee—you know, anything delicious. If I don't listen to my body, I will end up doubled over in a ball of great pain, cough constantly, or, what has happened more than I'd like to admit, even get sick and vomit. So I try to watch what I eat as much as possible.

But how is it possible that something so good could make me feel so bad? The Bible first gives us a glimpse of food in Genesis. God created plants and fruit trees for Adam and Eve to enjoy. "The earth brought forth vegetation, plants yielding seed according to their own kinds, and trees bearing fruit in which is their seed, each according to its kind" (1:12). And then he gave it *all* to Adam and Eve. "And God said, 'Behold, I have given you every plant yielding seed that is on the face of all the earth, and every tree with seed in its fruit. You shall have them for food" (verse 29). God doesn't give halfheartedly, and he doesn't give scraps or the leftovers. No, God was generous and lavishly gave them all they would need. He even made the food pleasant to look at (see 2:9). How amazing is that? Though God told Adam he was free to eat of the trees in the garden, the fruit of one tree was forbidden. And it was the fruit of that one tree that Adam and Eve couldn't resist. So every cough I have after a meal, every pain in my abdomen, every denial of certain foods is a reminder to me that the forbidden fruit was eaten.

The effects of the Fall on food and taste are enormous. Food spoils and rots, and some foods can develop dangerous bacteria such as salmonella and E. coli that can kill humans. Without food humans die. Too much food and we die. We can even die from drinking too much water—that's right, *water*. It's called water intoxication, and it is often fatal. Foods can be bitter to the taste or off-putting. I don't imagine anything was off-putting before the Fall. We can be allergic to foods, like peanuts and dairy. I need not go on. I imagine you've had some sort of struggle with food, if only a disdain for certain types or a tendency to eat too much of others. If you're one of those who do not like chocolate, I don't understand you. But I digress.

Even with all the detrimental effects of the Fall on food and taste, God continues to lavish his grace upon us. Sure, I must deny myself certain foods, but I also have the joy of broiling a six-ounce cut of salmon drizzled in olive oil and lemon pepper and then placing it on a bed of arugula and apples. I struggle with certain foods, but I still have an incredible amount of options. I don't mean to minimize the extremely difficult circumstances you may face with respect to dietary challenges. But I remember that God did create all these things for our enjoyment and delight. Even those of us who deal with restrictions generally have alternatives because of God's grace.

A SPIRITUALLY BALANCED DIET

Much of the trouble with appreciating the gift of food is due to struggles with idolatry. I know that word keeps coming up, but it's important for us to recognize how our tendency toward it undermines our ability to fully enjoy God's gifts. Some of us lean toward worshiping food, overeating, gluttony, and being consumed by what we eat, which can lead to disorders of the body and spirit. Anorexia and bulimia are serious medical conditions that require in-depth help, and therefore I won't explore them here. But I do want to consider the common experiences related to unhealthy attitudes toward this gift, such as denial, yo-yo dieting, and overeating.

Earlier I wrote that I have a love/hate relationship with food, and I'm guessing you might resonate with that perspective. "Experts" are constantly telling us what is healthy and what is not, what causes disease and what constitutes a "superfood"—only to say a few years later that their research was wrong. Butter is bad for you. Wait, no. Margarine is actually worse. Organic is best. Oh, but it also increases your risk of ingesting harmful bacteria. It's frustrating and confusing. And we are obsessed with it all.

If we eat a cookie, we feel guilty; if we don't eat a cookie, do we feel superior to those with less self-discipline? As one writer once said, "It's one thing to be careful about how you eat and cultivate your palate. But it's quite another when you can only drink just the right artisanal coffee (Starbucks isn't good enough anymore) or can't cope with a salad made with anything less than the freshest backyard-grown kale."[2] The person who desires backyard-grown kale is not sinful because of the desire for kale. We fall into sin when our hearts revolt against anything we consider inadequate or judge others who don't hold the same views. In other words, when food turns from being a delight and joy to being an idol or a measure of our own "goodness," that's when it's not good. Food cannot be truly enjoyed when it takes priority over the Bread of Life.

Puritan theologian Jonathan Edwards captured our struggle well:

> The wicked man, though he has the pleasures of this life, yet he partakes of them with fear. He lives in a slavish fear, all his days, of death and hell. He eats and drinks with fear, in fear, and this takes away much of the delight of what he enjoys. Though a man be rich and fares sumptuously, yet if he eats and drinks in fear of his life, this takes away all the comfort of his riches.[3]

As we struggle with food, it does take away all the joys and riches of enjoying this gift from God. But we are free to eat without fear or guilt when we enjoy food as a gift from God rather than the focus of our day.

Just as obsession with eating the "right" things can become idolatry, the same is true for gluttony—overeating. We can overeat for a variety of reasons including, but not limited to, depression and lack of contentment. Food can become something we turn to in an attempt to fulfill, comfort, and/or satisfy us. Food can become a trap and rule over us.

You might say, *Wait, I'm free to do whatever I want and eat whatever I desire. This isn't a matter worth taking up.* Paul heard this argument also, to which he responded, "'All things are lawful for me,' but not all things are helpful. 'All things are lawful for me,' but I will not be dominated by anything. 'Food is meant for the stomach and the stomach for food'—and God will destroy both one and the other" (1 Corinthians 6:12–13). Although Paul went on to address sexual immorality and the Corinthians' sexual appetites, the same warnings apply here for food. Everything is lawful, but not everything is beneficial. I want you to be free from the bondage of overeating and free to enjoy food. You and I must be reminded there is a better feast coming.

Jonathan Edwards had some more insights into our trouble with delight and eating:

> Any of the delights of this world are abundantly sweeter
> when taken temperately than when taken immoderately,
> as he that at a feast feeds with temperance has much
> greater pleasure of what he eats and drinks than he that
> gluts himself and vomits it up again. The godly have the
> prudence to take of earthly delights moderately, but the
> wicked man, he is unreasonable in it by being so greedy
> and violent, he presently loses the relish of his pleasure;
> but the godly takes those things so that the sweet relish of
> them remains all his lifetime.[4]

Edwards wasn't one to mince words, and what he said here is hard to read but true. When I gorge on food, I feel awful and I don't delight. It's a warning worth heeding. Let's not forget that eating is about delighting in God and delighting in the gifts from God. We can enjoy food and we can eat!

Finally, I know that some use food as a coping mechanism. Women joke often of getting through a miserable time or circumstance, such as a relational breakup, by eating a carton of ice cream or a pound of chocolate. It's a running joke, but so often it is the means by which we seek comfort. We must remember that God is the only One who can fill a void and satisfy completely. You and I must "taste and see that the LORD is good!" (Psalm 34:8). *Taste* here means to experience the great blessings of taking refuge in God. He is our satisfaction. What did the psalmist say? "Blessed is the man who takes refuge in him!" (34:8).

You can be like one of the five thousand who got their fill and then turned away and denied Jesus, or you can join the voice of Peter and proclaim, "Lord, to whom shall we go? You have the words of eternal life, and we have believed, and have come to know, that you are the Holy One of God" (John 6:68–69). As it relates to food, and any struggle, you and I must recognize there is no other place to turn.

FROM ENEMY TO JOY

My friend Becky[5] has a powerful testimony about her own love/ hate relationship with food, dating back to being what she calls "fairly chubby" as a child. "I hated the fact that most of my tiny little friends could eat whatever they wanted and still look like pixies," she told me, "while I wondered why my body just didn't look like theirs no matter how much I did or didn't eat. Food felt like my enemy." She explained that she had only a minimal understanding of the principles of nutrition. "I thought if I just ate a little *less,* everything would be okay," she said. "What I didn't understand was how important it was to monitor *what kind* of food I ate."

The gift in this adolescent struggle was that Becky learned to use food responsibly early in life. As she educated herself and experimented with different preparations and combinations of food, her perspective changed significantly over time. "Food and cooking were no longer my enemy," she said. Instead they became "a joyful gift to me—therapy of sorts, even. To me, food is (and should be recognized as) one of life's greatest love languages, both from God to us and from us to each other."

She continued, "Why do you suppose God gave us such a gorgeously diverse menu to choose from? I think he must have wanted us to have a delightful sensory adventure every time we eat. Why else would he create so many colors and textures and smells and flavors?"

As she mulled over the many possible reasons behind God's design of various aromas and flavors, Becky found that one rose to the top for her: "He loves his children. He delights in our enjoyment of his gifts to us—any and all of his gifts, including food."

And just as God created food out of love for us, she sees it as a beautiful resource we can use to love each other. "Few things express love more convincingly than learning a loved one's palate, seating them at our table, and delighting in a thoughtfully prepared meal complete with eye contact and meaningful conversation. It's an edible love letter."

I love Becky's insights and, like her, I'm so thankful God would provide such a brilliantly creative gift that we can receive with gratitude and share with joy, glorifying him each time we break bread with family and friends.

FASTING AND ENJOYING JESUS

Part of the beauty and joy of food actually comes from learning to deny ourselves of it in order to experience the fullness of our dependence on God. As we deny ourselves through fasting, we enjoy a deeper fellowship and communion with God. Ultimately, if we are going to think about enjoying all that God has for us in tasting, it would seem good to think about all that God has for us in resisting as well.

Fasting is one of the toughest Christian disciplines for me. I don't do it often, and frankly, it's because I don't think to do it. Fasting takes the kind of planning that, as an athlete, mother, and wife, I find incredibly difficult. Perhaps like me, you simply don't think about fasting. Eating is such a central part of our lives that denying ourselves of it for a time of prayer and meditation doesn't often come to mind. Or maybe it's never occurred to you to consider fasting as a means of drawing closer to God. I'm thankful the gospel frees me from the burden of disciplines in order to earn favor from God. In other words, fasting isn't a matter of salvation. But it is one of the practices the Lord encourages us to do. Both fasting and feasting are important aspects of the Christian life. Both help us reflect, honor, and worship God.

Because I know I'm not alone in this struggle, I'd like to take a beginner's look at fasting. (For an extensive look at fasting and the theology of it, I'd encourage you to read John Piper's book *A Hunger for God*.) Perhaps one of the first places to start is with Jesus himself. Have you ever noticed that Jesus didn't start his ministry as many of us begin ministry, jobs, and other major events? We might pray about it; perhaps we'll even get an entire group of friends to pray. But most of us don't have the thought, *I think I'll fast in a wilderness for forty days and forty nights.* Jesus did.

After Jesus finished his time of fasting, the devil came to tempt him. He first tried to use the fact that Jesus was hungry. He challenged Jesus to prove himself to be the Son of God by turning the stones to bread to feed himself. Jesus responded by saying, "Man shall not live by bread alone, but by every word that comes from the mouth of God" (Matthew 4:4). Jesus was able to fast because he was filled, so to speak, with the Word of God. He was filled with the Spirit of God (see 4:1).

I don't believe Christians must attempt forty-day fasts. I do, however, think the fact that Jesus fasted at all is a good indicator there's something unique and important to a time of denying ourselves of something that we crave or enjoy.

Later in his ministry, Jesus directly instructed us to fast, but I find it interesting that in his first instructions on fasting, instead of telling us how to do it, he informed us what *not* to do. Jesus told his followers to fast but not to look gloomy like the hypocrites did to be seen by others (see Matthew 6:16). He knows the human heart so well. He knows we will be tempted to desire praise from others for our efforts. He said that those who fast to be seen by others have already received their reward, so instead, fast in secret. God will know because he sees in secret (see verse 18). Fasting, like so many other topics we've covered in this book, is a matter of the heart.

Another thing I'd note is that Jesus didn't dictate what to fast from, how long to fast, or where to fast. It would seem the Christian is free to fast from whatever might be considered a sacrifice to give up. For you it might be social media, while for others it could be food. Twentieth-century preacher Martyn Lloyd-Jones put it this way:

> Fasting, if we conceive of it truly, must not . . . be confined to the question of food and drink; fasting should really be made to include abstinence from anything which is legitimate in and of itself for the sake of some special spiritual purpose. There are many bodily functions which are right and normal and perfectly legitimate, but which for special peculiar reasons in certain circumstances should be controlled. That is fasting.[6]

This is both freeing and convicting. I've so often used food as an excuse not to fast. I say things like, "I need to eat to serve my family, and I teach group fitness, so how can I fast?" But as you can see here, it's possible to experience fasting as a means for prayer and time to reflect on God without denying yourself food.

What do you think you might have trouble giving up for a period? Perhaps our answer to that question reveals the very thing you and I need to fast from.

I remember giving up coffee for a period of time. I went from drinking a cup a day with a sip every now and then in between to drinking nothing for several months. There came a point when I no longer craved it. I was completely satisfied not to have it again. But one day I decided to begin easing it back in. After the first sip I realized just how much I enjoyed the aroma of coffee and the warmth in my belly. I began to appreciate the joy of coffee drinking. I was more aware of the benefits—like getting a jolt of energy in the morning. I found greater delight in the flavor. Although I wasn't fasting from coffee for any spiritual reasons, it did make me more aware of the gift coffee can be, not only as something I enjoy, but also as the result of an image bearer's hard work in cultivating the land and picking the beans.

DELIGHTING IN THE GIFT OF FOOD

My prayer is that this chapter would open up a world of delight and joy with food. Apart from fasting, how do we learn to enjoy food? I think we begin by thanking God for all he has given to us. I'm writing this chapter around Thanksgiving. I've spent the past few weeks thinking about all that I am grateful for. The same should go for our food. As you look at the bounty of food, give thanks to God for his kind provision. Thank him for his creation. Thank him for the joy of delighting in all he has made and for the fact that you have dominion over it.

A part of thanksgiving is actually enjoying the food we eat. Eat, create, ponder, and *enjoy* what you are placing in your mouth. We often are rushed in eating. We run from place to place, grabbing what we can, or we eat dinner quickly because we must make it to the next thing. Our challenge is to try to savor our food. Paul exhorted us to be content and rejoice. We see this throughout the Scriptures but quite clearly in Philippians: "I know how to be brought low, and I know how to abound. In any and every circumstance, I have learned the secret of facing plenty and hunger, abundance and need" (4:12). A few verses earlier he told us to rejoice in the Lord always (see 4:4). If it's only a piece of bread, enjoy that piece of bread as if it were a rib-eye steak. Notice the texture, try to pick out the flavors, think of all that went into its creation, from the seed planted to the aroma of it baking, and thank God for the person who made the bread. There are many reasons and many ways for us to be thankful for that piece of bread. Let food go beyond simple nourishment.

And while we are eating and enjoying it, let's learn to break bread with others. When possible, allow people into your living space and enjoy a meal together. Hospitality is one practical way to show the love of Jesus, and what a simple way to enjoy one another! Cultivate your table for your family and close friends as well as welcoming strangers. If you have a family, attend to the needs of those closest to you during mealtime. Try to have meals together. Take that time to enjoy one another and reflect on what God is doing. As one leader wrote, "As the leader of my home I want the table to be a strategic intersection of our lives. It is a safe place. It is a place to express ideas, concerns, observations, emotions, and stories. That is, it is [a] place of intimacy."[7]

Remembering that Jesus is the Bread of Life makes me eager to participate in communion more fully. I want to take communion seriously. Church communion is one of the most special moments in worship for me, but it can also be a time when my mind is in a hundred places. I have to concentrate and pray. One of the most helpful practices I've found is to spend that time truly examining my heart and repenting of sin. It's an opportunity for me to reflect on the gospel and the sacrifice of Jesus on my behalf. Communion is a time of sober reflection, not to be taken casually or lightly.

The day is coming when you and I will never again fast; we will not hunger for God. We will be with him. We will enjoy him. And we will feast. Our weird food restrictions and aversions will be gone forever. We will no longer wrestle with gluttony or worry about eating too much—idolatry will be destroyed. We will feast and enjoy freely, purely. Think of those days ahead. They are coming. But until that day, God has given us much to enjoy and delight in, to taste and savor.

The Enjoy Project:
Taste and See

1. As we've seen in this chapter, food is a beautiful and wonderful gift, but it also can be the source of much sin, anguish, and discouragement. How have you struggled with enjoying food? Why?

2. Now that you've written or reflected on why it's hard to enjoy food, think about ways you can begin to enjoy it. Write down or reflect on them, and try to take action steps toward fighting what hinders you.

3. Fast. Fasting may be one of the most neglected practices in our Christian culture. If you are able to fast from food, do it in secret if possible. Use the time to pray and meditate on the Lord. Write or reflect on your experience. As noted in the chapter, if you cannot fast from food due to illness or other physical limitations, identify something that would be a sacrifice for you. For example, you might fast from breakfast only or from meat or sweets. As the Scriptures say, the goal is not to draw attention to self but to seek a deeper reliance on God.

4. Feast! Celebrate food. Cook a special meal. Eat at your favorite restaurant. Practice hospitality. Eat that dessert you've been wanting to try. Do whatever it is that would help you feast and thank God for taste. Perhaps all three meals of

one day could include your favorite dishes. Whatever you do, whether you eat or drink, do it to the glory of God. Enjoy!

5. Take someone a meal, or make a favorite meal for someone in your own family.

6. Look back over the chapter to identify one idea or truth that really stands out. Find a way to put that into practice this week.

7. Let's petition the Lord for all we need and thank him for his glorious provision of his Son. Pray and preach the gospel to yourself.

God, you are good, and your lavish generosity to me is so readily seen by the things that fill my plate. You've made me to depend on food for energy and life, and you graciously created food that delights my senses. Remind me that my dependence on food for physical life is a picture of my dependence on you for spiritual life. Thank you for Jesus, the Bread of Life, who alone can satisfy my deepest longings.

When we **eat,**

we **taste** the emblem of our

heavenly food—the

Bread of Life.

And when we **fast** we say,

"I *love* the *Reality*

above the emblem."

In the **heart of the saint**

both eating and fasting

are *worship.*

—John Piper

All Creation

Speaks His Name

You will rarely find me indoors if I don't have to be. My social media feeds are filled with pictures of me spending time outdoors, whether writing under a tree or riding my bike on a country road. God's creation is gorgeous to my eyes. I want to touch it, feel it, and though it makes me sneeze at times, smell it. I think one reason I'm so drawn to nature is that it reminds me of my Father.

Theologian John Calvin was noted by professor Stephen Nichols as saying that nature is "the theater of God's glory." Some might find musings on creation to be spiritually shallow. There is a temptation, I suppose, for some to completely ignore the beauty of nature, while others might worship it. Nichols explained,

> A naïve view [of nature and beauty] fails to connect with people, fails to match up with their sense of reality. Life is not always pretty flowers and rainbows. Consequently, we

should avoid a theology of nature and beauty that has no place for the fall. But we should equally avoid a view that has no place for beauty, for the goodness of creation.[1]

I get a sense that most of us probably are quite aware of the fallenness of creation, and later in this chapter we'll touch briefly on the stains and wrinkles that mar what once was Paradise. But for now, let's suspend that reality and immerse ourselves in the wonder that God created the world and made it beautiful.

GOD'S GLORY ON DISPLAY

We've read and gone over it, but it won't hurt to be reminded again just how significant it was that our Creator God gave us dominion over *his* creation. But beyond reflecting his love and care for us, creation establishes God's glory and power. In the beginning, God had the power to create whatever he wanted, however he desired. He is the supreme authority. He created everything. All the nature we enjoy, all the animals in the field, every living creature large or small came into being by the mind and word of God. He's incredibly creative! He is the Great I AM (see Exodus 3:14). In my opinion, we see these attributes and characteristics most clearly in and through creation.

Ultimately, creation displays the glory of God and preeminence of Christ (see Colossians 1:16). As pastor, theologian, and journalist Abraham Kuyper famously said, "Oh, no single piece of our mental world is to be hermetically sealed off from the rest, and there is not a square inch in the whole domain of our human existence over which Christ, who is sovereign over *all*, does not cry: 'Mine!'"[2]

I am fascinated by what Romans 1:20 suggests about God's glory revealed in creation: "For his invisible attributes, namely, his eternal power and divine nature, have been clearly perceived, ever since the creation of the world, in the things that have been made. So they are without excuse." I think as we look at creation, it takes more faith to believe there isn't a Creator than it does to believe there is. It's truly a sight to see.

Why is it that we are in awe of nature? Sure, we might find the sunset beautiful or the peak breathtaking, but what we are really in awe of is the Creator, whether we acknowledge it or not. One commentary, expounding on this scripture, said, "The entire natural world bears witness to God through its beauty, complexity, design, and usefulness."[3] But recognizing the reality of God through creation is not sufficient for salvation. For that, we must submit to the Creator as Lord. Church historian Stephen Nichols shared these insights while reflecting on the views of Jonathan Edwards: "It will take revelation, by which Edwards means scripture, to move one from a knowledge of God as Creator to knowledge of God as Savior, but Edwards begins with what all have been given: creation."[4]

In his kindness, God has universally given to all of us creation as a means to point to himself. We are without excuse. It is his common grace, goodness, and generosity that we can *all* enjoy creation, even without worshiping and believing in the One who created it.

But God does use nature at times to reveal his power and bring about the salvation of his people. When natural disasters strike, people often fall to their knees in prayer. I imagine some even place their faith in Jesus.

This reminds me of the story of Jonah. When I think of

Jonah, I immediately imagine my children's Bible and the vibrant pictures of a man in a whale. I thank God for the creative and useful way the writers of children's Bibles help bring the stories to life for my kids. I do, however, believe we sometimes risk trivializing the story of Jonah, viewing it as a fairy tale for children rather than the living Word of God for all. Jonah is a peculiar story and, if I'm honest, it takes great faith for me to imagine a man being swallowed by a fish. But this short book teaches us so much about God and why we can trust. I'd like to explore the sailors, whose role in Jonah's story is often overlooked.

The power of the sea is incredible. Can you imagine being out on a tempestuous body of water in a boat? And I'm not talking about a cruise ship. The boats in Jonah's time would have been much flimsier than what we imagine sailing on. The sea can be unpredictable, its vastness intimidating. I imagine the sailors of Jonah's day knew they were risking their lives every time they stepped onto the boat.

As a quick refresher, we know the Lord told Jonah to go to Nineveh and rebuke the people for their evil. Jonah, however, fled in the opposite direction, boarding a ship to Tarshish. Jonah, of course, couldn't escape God. The Lord caused a great storm on the sea. The mariners were afraid and immediately began to cry out to their various gods. Jonah, meanwhile, had gone down to the inner part of the ship and fallen asleep. Astonished to find him sleeping, the captain of the ship urged Jonah to arise and call out to his God. He said, "Perhaps the god will give a thought to us, that we may not perish" (1:6). The pagan sailors were afraid, desperate to know what they could do to save their lives. They cast lots to find out who was responsible for the storm. I find it remarkable that even these pagan sailors understood that someone greater than the wind would cause the storm. It reminds me of Romans 1:20.

Jonah told them that he was fleeing the presence of the Lord and that they should toss him overboard so they might be saved and the sea calmed. The men tried to row hard to get to land. Throwing Jonah overboard didn't appear to be their best first choice. But the sea continued to grow tempestuous, and they called out to the Lord, "O LORD, let us not perish for this man's life, and lay not on us innocent blood, for you, O LORD, have done as it pleased you" (1:14). They picked Jonah up and hurled him over.

We know the rest. Jonah was swallowed by the fish, and eventually he repented. But before that, have you ever noticed this amazing transformation? The writer of Jonah noted that the sailors "feared the LORD exceedingly, and they offered a sacrifice to the LORD and made vows" (1:16).

These were changed men. First, they acknowledged the power and sovereignty of God in verse 14. I imagine they would have echoed the words of Jeremiah 32:17, "Ah, Lord GOD! It is you who have made the heavens and the earth by your great power and by your outstretched arm! Nothing is too hard for you." Then what was once a fear for their lives and a fear of the seas turned into a fear of the Lord. And they didn't fear the Lord just a little but exceedingly—they were new creations. The fear of the Lord produced reverence and awe, so they rightly offered a sacrifice and began to worship. What a powerful example of the Lord using nature, along with the sin of Jonah, to display his glory and mercy. (Ironically, it was because of God's mercy that Jonah was fleeing. Jonah didn't want God to have mercy on the people of Nineveh. God is *exceedingly* good and merciful!)

CREATION GROANS

Even as we acknowledge the power of God on display in nature, it's important to consider how the Fall affected creation and twisted its perfect beauty in profound ways.

I live in Tennessee, home of incredible allergy-producing plants and trees. CNN reported that two of our state's major cities made the Asthma and Allergy Foundation's annual list of the ten worst places for spring allergy sufferers.[5] I was raised in Knoxville, Tennessee, the top on that list.

Thankfully, while I sneeze on occasion, I seem to be mostly immune to the allergies that cause some to have itchy eyes, scratchy throats, and hay fever. I don't remember ever struggling much, but I've had plenty of friends who do. I'm sharing this because as wonderful as nature is, I do acknowledge that for you, it might actually be quite miserable.

God never intended for us to step outside and begin sneezing or wheezing. You and I should be able to enjoy nature without the fear of getting a poison ivy rash, being stung by a bee (one of my great fears), or getting struck by lightning. These are all results of the Fall. It's the horrible curse of all things. Creation is where God loves to reveal himself, but it is also fraught with evidence of the Fall.

Mold, decay, and death all point to a world that isn't as it should be. We know this. But I find it amazing that humans aren't the only ones waiting and longing for all things to be made new. Romans informs us that creation waits, and it does so with eager longing (see 8:19).

Without getting too graphic, something about the longing and waiting for the return of Jesus reminds me of childbirth. Childbirth is painful and filled with groaning, including the nine months of waiting. It's an intense process. Paul used this analogy when he wrote, "For we know that the whole creation has been groaning together in the pains of childbirth until now" (verse 22). Until the Lord returns, creation will continue to groan and feel the pains of the Fall. I'll explore this further in a later chapter as we look to heaven, but for now, as we wait, we wait and long with hope. We have a hope of the future glory. We wait and long and learn to enjoy in the present age until all things are made right.

GOD'S DELIGHT IN CREATION

Have you ever read a book a second time and discovered something new or recognized a new twist or character that you hadn't noticed before? Some stories just get sweeter each time you read them. You know the end of the story, but you simply can't put it down. That's how I often feel when reading the Psalms, and that perfectly describes my experience as I recently reread Psalm 104. Had I only skimmed this beautiful hymn of praise in the past? I read it and each verse seemed to build upon the next:

- the Lord is great (verse 1);
- he sets the earth in its place and it stays (verse 5);
- the voice of the Lord has power to move wind and mountains (verses 7–8);
- he makes springs flow by hillsides and through valleys (verse 10);
- birds sing in the heavens (verse 12);
- the earth is satisfied with the fruit of his work (verse 13);
- he causes grass to grow for livestock and plants for man to cultivate (verse 14);

- he makes man's heart glad through his provision (verse 15);
- the moon and sun know what they are made for and how to work properly (verse 19); and so on.

In verse 24 it's almost as if the writer was overcome by all that the Lord has done: "O LORD, how manifold are your works! In wisdom have you made them all; the earth is full of your creatures." Yes, the Lord is awesome and amazing. "Bless the LORD, O my soul! Praise the LORD!" (verse 35).

God not only cares greatly for his creation but he also sustains it. Verse 5 stopped me in my tracks: "He set the earth on its foundations, so that it should never be moved." At the strangest times I'll have this thought: *What if the earth falls from the sky?* It blows my mind that the earth and everything in our galaxy and beyond is suspended in a massive blank space of darkness. I took astronomy in college. I don't remember much about it except that it was the only course in which I received a C during my college education! Needless to say, I didn't take the second half of that course. What I do remember from astronomy class is feeling quite small. The expanse of the universe is immeasurable. It's enormous and awe inspiring. I don't understand the physics of it all, but I do know that God has made it so. He is awesome and powerful. In his goodness and grace he holds all things together—ultimately for his glory but also because he delights in what he has made.

A theme you can't escape throughout Psalm 104 is God's abundant care and provision for the earth and all that is within it.

Three months into our marriage, my husband and I woke up one Saturday and decided to go and get a puppy. It was one of the most spontaneous and joy-filled things we've done. We immediately began to look for people who sold purebred English Springer Spaniels. To this day I have no idea why we got so specific. I imagine the breed was my husband's idea. We found someone, called, and within an hour or two of our deciding to purchase a dog, Ollie was sitting in my lap as we drove home.

We looked at each other and realized we now needed to purchase *a lot* of things to care for him. The breeder had given us a few items, so we had a little time to prepare. We bought a crate to make sure he traveled safely, lots of food, a leash, a few chew toys, a little fence, and a small bed. We got his shots and made sure he had tick and flea repellent. When we went out of town, if someone wasn't watching him, we made sure he was secure in a place that would care for animals while their owners were away. We sure loved him. Once we had our first child, however, the amount of love and care we had showered on Ollie paled in comparison. And our love for our kids pales in comparison to God's love for us, our children, and all his creation.

Of all God's creation, man is the only one he designates as made in his image. You and I have a privileged place in the creation order that, considering our sinful hearts, should cause us to be filled with gratitude and humility. Of course, that's not always my response. I get easily distracted by the cares of this world. But when I do sit back, when I have those moments of heart-pounding gratefulness and worship, Psalm 8 reminds me of God's amazing love and grace. I say with the psalmist, "When I look at your heavens, the work of your fingers, the moon and the stars, which you have set in place, what is man that you are mindful of him, and the son of man that you care for him?" (verses 3–4). Seriously! When you truly consider all that God has done, his power and his greatness, you can't help but wonder why he'd be so very mindful of man. He clothes the lilies of the fields and then makes sure we know that he will even more completely care for us. He isn't going to cut any corners, so we can rest and not be anxious (see Matthew 6:25–34). He's so mindful that he sent his Son to die for us. His gift and care don't make us proud; they make us fall on our faces. We can join with the psalmist and proclaim, "O LORD, our Lord, how majestic is your name in all the earth!" (Psalm 8:9).

Like all the wonders of this earth, you and I are also created. God said in his Word that he knitted you together in your mother's womb (see Psalm 139:13). Every fiber, every blood vessel, all those millions of cells, every molecule of DNA is designed and created by God. That's incredible. Smiles and laughter—God created that jovial noise and that beautiful expression. All the various colors of skin—God had that in mind. My face is covered with freckles, and I'd like to think those childlike dots aren't a result of the Fall but God's design.

Certainly there are things that happen and change in our bodies as a result of the Fall. Wrinkles, though beautiful as a sign of wisdom, are also a sign of aging. Aging brings with it aches that were never meant to be, possible memory loss, and ultimately, death. Christians, however, don't look to the aging process with hopelessness and agony. We know it is bringing us closer to our Savior. But the reality is that our fallen bodies sometimes do get in the way of enjoyment. Sickness that leads to the flu, one sleepless night that leads to frequent insomnia, a small lump that leads to a cancerous tumor; all these things shouldn't be what our bodies experience. But just as creation groans and waits, we too groan and wait for that day when he will make all things new, including our bodies (see 1 Corinthians 15:42–53).

As you delight in creation, let yourself consider how God delights in you. Zephaniah reminds us that the Lord is mighty to save and he rejoices over you with gladness and exults over you with loud singing (see 3:17). God isn't far off. He is near and he loves you dearly—his created daughter. He cares greatly for nature, but do not forget that he also cares for and delights in you. Isn't it amazing?

OUR CARE FOR CREATION

God's great care for us is one motivator to care for what he has given to us. God gave humanity dominion over creation and instructed us to subdue the earth. Some take this to mean we are free to do whatever we wish with creation. We actually are called to care for it and make it useful for ourselves. Any abuse of creation isn't a result of God's command to subdue it but rather a result of the Fall.

To have dominion over the earth is a responsibility, not only a gift. We must recognize that it still remains *his* creation. Again, I love how Stephen Nichols explained what he calls ecotheology: "An ecotheology also entails an ethic of cultivation over and against the ethic of 'consumption' that drives so much of Western culture. As stewards of the creation we should be concerned with cultivating natural resources."[6]

You and I should care for, steward, and cultivate the earth. God loves his creation; he called it good. He delights in it. You and I are called to echo that delight as we care for it. Our care is not propelled by a worship of creation but is an act of worship of the One who made it. Each of us must decide in our own minds and hearts what that care will look like. Certainly at the most basic level such care would mean obeying the laws of the land regarding littering, hunting, polluting, and other laws meant to help preserve creation.

When I was in high school, several times a bunch of us kids would pick up trash and litter from the sides of the roads as a service project. Recycling is another practical way to preserve the earth that God has entrusted to us, as is composting, which my family has experimented with.

Let your imagination run wild as you consider ways to enjoy the earth through both consumption and care as a means of honoring the God who created it.

DELIGHTING LIKE CHILDREN

If you have young kids and live in or near a city, you probably have a zoo pass. Even if you don't have a season pass, you'll likely at some point find yourself packing lunches and water, hoping it doesn't rain, and getting a stroller ready for the long walk around the zoo, if only for one day.

Each year our family gets a season pass because we know we'll go to the zoo at least twice, if not several more times in the season, and season passes are more cost effective than individual tickets. Each time we go, I get anxious as I think about how long we'll potentially be there. I tend to skip exhibits, reroute the kids so we don't have to stop at a certain playground, try to convince them they really don't want to go into the petting zoo, and tell them when it's time to move on. (Babies, if you ever read this, I love you and I'm so sorry!) It's shameful. But it's true. It's typically motivated by the simple fear of eating up an entire day at the zoo—nothing more than selfishly not wanting to devote more than a few hours to looking at the animals. Not that there's a problem with having a schedule and adhering to it. But for me, the zoo could be a wonderful opportunity to help my kids learn to delight and enjoy what God has made, but instead of concentrating on that in the past, I've consistently thought about the time. Thankfully, God is gracious to reveal to me my tendencies and help me grow and change.

But even as I wrestle to maintain the right attitude, I notice that kids have a way of teaching us to enjoy and reflect. When my kids go to the zoo, they want to stop and read every sign about each animal. They want to know what it eats and whether it's nocturnal. They patiently wait to see if it will move. Honestly, as they watch the animals I often find myself transfixed by their wide-eyed wonder and oohs and aahs. When I'm not anxiously trying to move on to the next exhibit, I'm learning from them. It's beautiful and opens up wonderful conversations about God's creativity.

I want to grow in my wonder. You and I need eyes to see the beauty of everyday life. I want to pause more often than not, stare at the bees buzzing near the flowers, take in the beauty of creation, and play in it. That beautiful sunset reflects the beauty and majesty of God. And as God delights and rejoices over me, I'd like to delight and rejoice over what he has created for me.

The Enjoy Project:
All Creation Speaks His Name

1. What have been your views on creation and how it relates to God and humanity?

2. In what ways has your view of creation hindered your enjoyment of it? Do you tend to either ignore its significance or get caught up in its beauty without acknowledging the Creator? How might you seek to better delight in creation?

3. Go outside for a period of time, perhaps thirty minutes to one hour. If health or other issues make this impossible, grab a seat by a window or find images of nature in a book or on the Internet. Without music or other distractions, look for signs of God revealing himself through nature. Think of what is beautiful: the various sounds, colors, fragrances. How do these things point to God, and what do they reveal to you about his character?

4. Either go outside or reflect back on a time when you were in nature. How did that experience delight your senses?

5. Part of our purpose as created human beings is to subdue and exercise dominion over the earth. We know that God cares for his creation. What is one way you might practically care for creation? Seek to do that this week.

6. Look back over the chapter to identify one idea

or truth that really stands out. Find a way to put that into practice this week.

7. Creation screams of the glory and beauty of God! Read and pray through Psalm 8. Pray and preach the gospel to yourself.

Thank you, Father, that I am surrounded by creation that screams of your beauty and glory. From the most magnificent galaxy to the smallest intricately designed insect, all of it reveals your majesty. Like David I cry, "What is man that you are mindful of him?" And yet you gave Jesus to be the rescuer for me. There is no question of your love. Along with the rest of creation, I praise and lift you high.

There is not one

blade of grass,

there is no

color in this world

that is not intended to

make us rejoice.

—John Calvin

The Art of Life

*I*t's interesting how something can be so central to your everyday life at one time and then gradually fade away. We see this with friendships. I had friends in my younger years who I thought would be friends forever, and though we continue to have mutual respect, we no longer communicate. Life happened and we moved to new cities, got married, attended different churches, and simply grew apart. It wasn't intentional; it just happened. Similarly, somehow over the years my relationship with the arts has nearly vanished.

Many of my friends now would be surprised to know I played the flute and piccolo from middle school through my freshman year of college. I was a member of the Pride of the Southland Marching Band at the University of Tennessee and played in the pep band for the Lady Vols basketball team. To say I was committed would be an understatement. I practiced and enjoyed it. Now, however, I get my flute out only when one of my kids asks to see mommy play, when they want to play with it themselves, and during the holidays because I love to play Christmas music.

I was also a dancer and cheerleader—committed and

competitive in each. I actually competed in a small ballroom dance competition a few years into my marriage. I simply loved to dance and found a new and exciting form in which to enjoy it. I also studied abroad and remember standing in awe of the work of French sculptor Auguste Rodin, perhaps most famous for his work *The Thinker*. And I've seen more musicals than I can count. The arts, in one way or another, played an integral role in my life for many years.

I'm not sure what happened or when, but at some point I forgot how much I enjoyed music, I forgot that dance was something I delighted in, and I forgot how beautiful art could move me to delight. I imagine the transition came with the arrival of our children. With a few rare exceptions, it seemed my music selection went from Ella Fitzgerald and B. B. King to "The Itsy Bitsy Spider." Our movie choices changed. Dance was limited to "Ring Around the Rosie" and the "Hokey Pokey." Theater—what's that? I simply didn't feel I had time to devote to those things any longer.

Over the past few years, the Lord has not only reignited my love for the arts but also helped me see how I can include my kids by teaching them to enjoy the arts for his glory.

PORTRAIT OF THE ARTIST

In the creation account, we know that God created every human being in his image. He did not distinguish between believers and unbelievers. Those who do not worship him, and may never worship him, still have the capacity to reflect the Lord's image with their various gifts and talents. There isn't anything we have that was not first given, whether or not we acknowledge it (see 1 Corinthians 4:7). One effect of God's common grace is that art doesn't need to be explicitly Christian in order to be enjoyed. We can appreciate it as a reflection of God's beauty and character simply because it was created by one of his image bearers. We must believe this in order to be free to enjoy the arts without guilt.

In many ways, this entire book is a call to see and know that God gives good gifts and is the Giver of all things good, whether it's food, skills, or the ocean. The risk to our souls is in how we view the gifts. Do we avoid them in fear or ingratitude, or do we allow them to consume our attention to the point of idolatry? Or do we choose to delight in how they reveal to us something important about God? Think of how much more delightful the arts would be if we recognized the Giver of the gift. I am of the belief that there's no "natural" ability. I believe every good and perfect gift comes from the Father. That's why we want to resist the temptation to dismiss the value of the arts in our spiritual lives.

My daughter and I recently saw a local performance of *The Nutcracker*. At one point, when the prince took the girl up in the air, my daughter's eyes got wide and her mouth dropped. She whispered, "That's awesome!" My young baby girl wouldn't think to attribute such beauty to the Lord, but I knew. I knew that what she was experiencing wasn't merely the beauty of the dancers but the beauty of their Creator. God created us with senses, hearts, and minds that are built to respond to beautiful things, whether mountains, music, or movement. The fact that we have the ability to move in such a way that inspires is only because of God. My little girl was experiencing this reality.

We are all at one time or another like my daughter, gasping at the beauty of God's creation—the artist who takes solid colors and blends them into a tapestry of trees and flowers that look as if you could walk right into the page. The dancer who can spin on his head without breaking his neck. The marathon runner who can run for miles without stopping or even looking tired. Although I don't have a chapter dedicated to athletes, we cannot deny the art-like gifts and skills needed to perform a sport. There's an art to runners' breathing, the form of their running styles, the way God created them with tiny frames and lung capacities that can endure miles and miles of bounding and deep, slow, and steady breaths. What about the illustrator who uses pixels to create a character, like Buzz or Woody, that is etched in our memories forever? These are people who often take our breath away. God has made them to do marvelous things, and we delight in the result of their gifts. As we enjoy these beautiful things, we know it is God who made it so.

As Christians, we have an opportunity to use our art to bring glory to God. It doesn't have to be explicitly Christian, but we can certainly point others to the Creator and can mirror what is true, honorable, just, pure, lovely, commendable, and excellent (see Philippians 4:8). Theologian and philosopher Francis Schaeffer wrote, "A Christian should use these arts to the glory of God, not just as tracts, mind you, but as things of beauty to the praise of God. An art work can be a doxology in itself."[1] The art we create and the art we enjoy can point to God and his beauty.

Whether it's through the poetry in the Psalms or the worship leader at our church or the ballerina dancing en pointe, art is designed to remind us of our Creator God. In addition, the arts are valuable to us because they are valuable to God. God has invested in the creature who is creating. God created beautifully, and one way we can reflect and image him is to beautifully create as well. But art is truly beautiful and can be fully enjoyed only when it doesn't cause us to sin or isn't sinful in nature.

DISCERNMENT IN ART APPRECIATION

As with all God's good gifts, the Fall has the potential to corrupt our enjoyment of the arts. Art can tempt us to sin in lust, anger, and even fear. Pornography is one of the obvious contenders here. Though we can't really call it art, some try to justify it on the grounds of artistic expression and appreciation. But we don't have to go toward the extreme to corrupt something that was meant to glorify God. Our lustful thoughts can take a beautiful ballet and make it sexual, for example. There's wisdom in knowing your weaknesses and the boundaries you must set to avoid temptation, even if others think they are ridiculous or accuse you of being a prude.

I'm intentionally not sharing the specific boundaries that I set. We must each be convinced in our own minds and listen to the guidance of the Holy Spirit. Much about the arts is what some might call a gray area that God doesn't specifically address. I don't want to share extrabiblical guidelines that you might adopt as a way to think and live. In other words, some of my convictions in this area don't necessarily apply to everyone. And some of my liberties could be a stumbling block for my sisters. God cares about your heart, not superficial rules that lead to Pharisaical superiority or that justify and feed hedonistic appetites. Even something that's beautiful can also play on our emotions in ways that, at some times in our lives, we aren't ready to handle. If you're in a depression, for example, watching *Schindler's List* may not be wise—but few would call it sinful. Something like that requires discernment and leading from the Holy Spirit, and a set of rules that I might have would not prove helpful.

There are, however, two things God clearly warns against that apply to the arts: idolatry and worldliness.

Idolatry

An announcement for a new "bible" recently caught my eye. Developed and created by fans of a famous rapper, this "bible," which isn't endorsed or created by the artist, is a travesty. The reason? Every instance where you'd normally read the word *God* has been replaced with the artist's name. I don't know the motives of the creators of this book; perhaps one is simply to make a buck. But this does shine light on the culture of celebrity that tends to emerge within the arts, to the point of idolatry. We must assume that the writers of this book aren't believers. If they are, I pray someone will be loving enough to speak truth into their lives. But is there any lesson to be learned for us as it applies to our appreciation and enjoyment of the arts? There are a few, but I think what we must consider is our own tendency to idolize the creature rather than the Creator.

God's Word has much to say about idolatry, but for the most succinct statements we can go straight to the commandments:

> You shall have no other gods before me. You shall not make for yourself a carved image, or any likeness of anything that is in heaven above, or that is in the earth beneath, or that is in the water under the earth. (Exodus 20:3–4)

As you've likely seen throughout this book, the heart is prone to idolatry, to letting something or someone replace God in our thoughts, hearts, and actions. We are called to love God with all our hearts and minds. When passion for something other than the Lord—whether victory for our favorite sports team, skill to excel in our art, or tickets to a particular concert—begins to consume us, it's idolatry. When we forget God created that individual with certain gifts that ultimately point to God as the Giver of good things, we can develop an unhealthy obsession with the person or the art form. We won't likely make a "bible," but it can indeed control us.

That could look like being offended when an artist doesn't provide an autograph or becoming irritable when you miss the chance to watch a game on television. If upon learning that we may not be able to pursue our art in the ways we'd hoped for, how we respond may reveal if we idolize the art form. Perhaps we've placed our identity in writing, keeping our home beautiful, dancing, singing, or playing football. If finances, health, or other obstacles prevent us from fulfilling our dreams, we may fall into self-pity, resentment, and anger. There are a number of ways we might idolize the art or the artist over the Creator.

One way to guard against this temptation to idolize our heroes is by remembering that our heroes will indeed fail us. One of my all-time favorite television stars, who made great history in television and helped dispel many stereotypes of the African American family, fell from grace in the public eye. It was devastating and yet another reminder that my hope can never be placed in a person. I imagine you can think of many similar examples. This should lead us to pray for protection, wisdom, grace, and salvation where needed for our heroes instead of worshiping them.

The good news for this temptation to idolatry is that we are never too far off from the reach of our awesome and mighty God.

There is hope for us. God's Word contains the words of life, and we can trust that what God says is true. His promise, even as we fight off our idols, is to finish the good work he began in us. But there's no denying there's a fight. We can't simply read our Bibles and hope for change—we must pursue it.

Worldliness

One all-too-common attitude is that since we no longer live under the burden of legalism, we are free to partake in any activity without regard for any moral or ethical concerns. Again, our convictions may vary, but some forms of entertainment clearly do not honor God. The literary erotica *Fifty Shades of Grey* phenomenon comes to mind. Women, Christian women included, flocked to the book. The world was taking part, and many didn't want to miss out on whatever was causing all the buzz.

But for those of us who didn't join in the *Fifty Shades* phenomenon, let's not be too quick to pat ourselves on the back. Plenty of other media choices can tempt us to lust, envy, and in short, adopt worldly values. *Fifty Shades,* since it is essentially soft pornography, is a clear example, but you may want to challenge yourself to discern what other forms of media (television, movies, and music) cause you to struggle.

God anticipated and warned against the temptation toward worldliness. In 1 John 2:15–16 we read, "Do not love the world or the things in the world. If anyone loves the world, the love of the Father is not in him. For all that is in the world—the desires of the flesh and the desires of the eyes and pride of life—is not from the Father but is from the world."

We know that God loves the world (see John 3:16), so it would be unwise to take these verses to mean we must never be *in* the world. What we must guard against is being *of* the world. Being *of* the world means to take its values and priorities as our own. And by *world*, John meant those things that would be against the Lord.

If you and I have the Spirit of God within us, we must listen to those promptings that might say, *No, don't watch this. It will not benefit your soul.* We must not suppress those nudges or fight against them. They are a gift from God meant for our good and our protection.

If we truly believe all that the Bible says about Jesus and his sacrifice on the cross, then we will fight the desires of the flesh. As Paul said in Romans 6:1–2, "What shall we say then? Are we to continue in sin that grace may abound? By no means! How can we who died to sin still live in it?" Right before these verses, Paul shared about the abundant grace of God given to us because of Jesus's death and resurrection (see 5:18–21). The grace that we have obtained is amazing and unmerited favor. So when faced with a temptation to be led by the world and the desires of the flesh, we must decide whether we will abuse the grace of God or walk in love.

What we consume will bear consequences, from broken relationships to addiction to pornography to distraction from the life of beauty we are meant to enjoy. By contrast, various media and art can magnify the glory of the Lord in our eyes. We can grow in appreciation for how he has created others. We can enjoy the gifts and talents of our neighbors. Some things can help us relax and rest. Our consumption can produce joy and even peace; we simply want to be wise and careful. We also can remember these words from John: "And the world is passing away along with its desires, but whoever does the will of God abides forever" (1 John

2:17). It's all passing away, and so will our sinful desires. That's such a relief! We won't fight the good fight of faith forever. One day we won't have to wrestle with what is a gray area and what is good. We will simply enjoy God and all that he has for us in heaven forever.

A LIFE OF BEAUTY AND STRENGTH

There are a number of ways we can pursue the arts in a God-glorifying manner. First, let's begin to recognize God and his beauty as we enjoy or participate in the various arts available to us. God is beautiful, and every melody and harmony, arabesque and pirouette, Picasso and Monet points to his beauty. We can encourage and instruct the children in our lives by telling them their artistic and creative abilities come from their Creator God. What a wonderful opportunity for us to point our children ultimately to Jesus and to remind *ourselves* of this truth.

I marvel at the thought that the Lord created sound waves that lead to bass notes that come out of the diaphragm of a human being. Who could think to create a place to live that towers over a village, probably includes a gate, and has several pointed edges at the top of its features and call it a castle? To me a quilt is just a blanket, but to the one who created it, it's a tapestry of patterns, each carefully considered to create a covering that ultimately reflects the God who created her. I want to view the world from that angle: this isn't just a sound or a building or a quilt but a reflection of our Creator God. God created colors and textures and all things beautiful. Let's open our eyes, hearts, and senses to experience it.

We can also transform the way we think about surrounding ourselves with beautiful things, whether purchased or made to reflect our own creativity. Once we put God into the equation, decorating, for example, isn't merely decorating but an opportunity to reflect his beauty through the environment we create in our homes. Of course, this shouldn't become a burden in your already busy life. In other words, if decorating isn't one of your gifts or something you desire to invest much time in, that is fine. The point is simply that when we do make things beautiful in our homes, we can do so in ways that reflect our Savior. And ultimately it's a tiny taste of the glorious heaven we will one day live in forever. Won't it be nice not to need to clean but instead to be able to forever enjoy the beauty of our eternal home?

Another way we can reflect God and enjoy the arts is through creating and even market making. Sites like Etsy and Pinterest come to mind. I am not on either site and am not particularly gifted in this way, but I can definitely see the beauty in a three-tiered cake that looks like a castle. I may not be able to make it, but I can encourage the women around me who are able to create beautiful things out of flour and sugar. I can do this because I know God has given them that ability and it is beautiful.

Go to the movies, listen to the symphony, head to the basketball game with new and fresh eyes. God has done such beautiful things. Let's look on, receive this gift, and give thanks.

The Enjoy Project:
The Art of Life

1. What are some things that hinder you from enjoying the arts?

2. We want to cultivate a love for the arts because they point to our Creator God. What are ways you see God reflected in the various arts?

3. Are there certain ways the arts have tempted you to sin, whether films you later wish you hadn't seen or books that weren't edifying? What changes might you consider making as a result?

4. Is there a certain art you enjoy participating in or have wanted to try? Find a way to do it this week or over the course of the month. Maybe you want to take a cooking class, take ballroom dance lessons, try painting, listen to music, or dance in your living room. It doesn't have to be elaborate, but find a way to incorporate it into your schedule.

5. Is there a certain art you enjoy experiencing, one which you appreciate how others express their gifts? Find an opportunity to enjoy that art and reflect on how God can be glorified in that form of expression. What does that particular art say about God? You may end up repeating an activity from item 4, such as listening to music, but this could also be going to an art museum, attending a play, heading to an

outdoor music festival, or some other event
where people's gifts are on display.

6. Look back over the chapter to identify one idea
   or truth that really stands out. Find a way to put
   that into practice this week.

7. Pray and preach the gospel to yourself.

*Out of your great love and generosity,
God, you've made me to image you in the
ability to create unique and beautiful things.
Help me to see a colorful painting, hear a
beautiful song, and watch a stirring play and
recognize how you are glorified through them.
Keep my heart from becoming callous,
idolizing the one who has been gifted instead
of glorifying you, the good Giver. Thank you
for this gracious, extravagant gift.*

The *Lord* doesn't like us
to be dead. **Be alive.** . . .

Sometimes I *dance*

to the *glory* of the *Lord,*

because He said so.

—Mahalia Jackson

Delighting in the Giver

*T*hroughout this book we've explored delighting in a variety of things but all with the intent that, as we pursue and involve ourselves in relationships, food, nature, and all the other wonderful gifts God has given us, you and I would learn how to enjoy God, acknowledging him as the Giver of all good things. This has to be a deliberate choice because we tend toward an attitude of consumerism in which we just take what's been made available to us. But when we pause and learn to delight in these areas, we also learn to delight in God and give proper thanks and admiration. We can worship God while preparing a meal, riding a bike, or listening to a symphony. We delight and give thanks not solely because he gives good gifts but also because he is God.

Over the past fifteen years and certainly before I set out to write this chapter, I would easily have claimed to have always enjoyed God to one degree or another. The thought of struggling to be glad in God—to find contentment in knowing him and his goodness and rejoicing in that—was really foreign to me. Have I always rejoiced in suffering or difficult circumstances perfectly? No. But more times than not, I would have been able to fight through to faith. This particular season, however, was the first time I struggled to do so.

Thanksgiving and Christmas were just around the corner, and I knew this season would be a time of both rejoicing and sorrows. My husband and I had experienced losses in our family—both of our older siblings had passed away. The holidays seemed uniquely grim to me this year. I wasn't looking forward to all the rejoicing that I knew would be going on around me, but more than that, I was struggling to remember God's character. If God is good, why do so many hard things happen?

I could tell you all the theological answers. But I needed more than words—even the good gift of God's Word, which we will explore soon. I needed the gift of faith that would come only from the Giver of good gifts—God himself. I prayed like never before and doubted like never before. One of the things I kept remembering was that God says he will finish the good work he began in me. If God's Word is true, then regardless of how much I doubt, he's not going to leave me there.

As always, the Lord proved faithful. After several months of lamenting, which felt like a decade, the Lord brought me out of that dark season and gave me fresh faith. Why am I sharing this with you? Because I know the idea of finding joy in God and delighting in him might seem difficult at times, maybe even most times. Your circumstances or feelings may be clouding the truth of God's Word. You may not sense his nearness. I understand. There were moments when I wasn't even sure I was a Christian. But then the Lord would cause me to fall on my knees yet again in prayer, crying out to him—reconfirming to me that he has me in the palm of his hand. I'm his daughter, and he will never let me go.

Sometimes God lets us come to the end of ourselves in order for us to enjoy more of him. That makes sense to me. When there's nowhere else to run, we can run to our Savior. As we look to what it means to enjoy God, we are, in many ways, also losing ourselves. We gain something far greater when we are most concerned and obsessed with the One we'll be concerned and obsessed with for all eternity.

THE CHIEF END OF MAN

What's your purpose? What's most important to you in life? As I shared in the first chapter, *The Westminster Catechism* states that the "chief end of man" is "to glorify God, and to enjoy him for ever."[1] We'll be worshiping him forever—for all eternity. We want to enjoy God not solely because he gives us good things but because he is God and worthy of our admiration, worship, affection, and thanksgiving.

If that's the chief end, our purpose for living, how do we do it? We start with enjoying the things that matter to God.

The Beloved Son

One cannot speak of enjoying God without contemplating what it means to enjoy Jesus. Jesus is his Father's delight and joy. He is the center of Christianity, the focus of the Bible, the reason for our joy and worship. In Michael Reeves's excellent book *Rejoicing in Christ,* he said,

> Jesus Christ, God's perfect Son, is the Beloved of the
> Father, the Song of the angels, the Logic of creation, the
> great Mystery of godliness, the bottomless Spring of life,

comfort and joy. We were made to find our satisfaction, our heart's rest, in him.[2]

Yes! He is the spring of life. Our life and worship are all about him and for him. Reeves continued,

> The center, the cornerstone, the jewel in the crown of Christianity is not an idea, a system or a thing; it is not even "the gospel" as such. It is Jesus Christ. He is not a mere topic, a subject we can pick out from a menu of options. Without him, our gospel or our system— however, coherent, "grace-filled" or "Bible-based"— simply is not Christian.[3]

If you want God, you must also want Jesus. If you want to truly know God, you must truly know Jesus. The only way to the Father is through the Son (see John 14:6). God loves his Son, his Beloved. God made sure to let Jesus know the depths of his love during his baptism when, as he came up from the water, the Spirit of God descended like a dove and a voice from heaven said, "This is my beloved Son, with whom I am well pleased" (Matthew 3:17).

This makes me think about the wonderful celebration of my baptism. My father couldn't be there because he had passed away, but I imagine he would have been pleased. My father loved me dearly and always rejoiced over me. He was a man who supported and encouraged well. My father's love, though great, pales in comparison with the Father's love for his Son, Jesus.

If God delights in Jesus, surely we ought to as well. Thank him, praise his name, sing to him. Paul's reflections and praise of

Christ in the first part of Colossians captures to me all that he is:

> He is the image of the invisible God, the firstborn of all
> creation. For by him all things were created, in heaven and
> on earth, visible and invisible, whether thrones or
> dominions or rulers or authorities—all things were
> created through him and for him. And he is before all
> things, and in him all things hold together. And he is the
> head of the body, the church. He is the beginning, the
> firstborn from the dead, that in everything he might be
> preeminent. For in him all the fullness of God was pleased
> to dwell, and through him to reconcile to himself all
> things, whether on earth or in heaven, making peace by
> the blood of his cross. (1:15–20)

Paul echoed the words of John, who said Jesus was there with God in the beginning. He was the Word and was God, and all things were made through him (see 1:1–3). Jesus has authority. And yet he became Emmanuel (God with us), and he died and rose and is seated at the right hand of God, where he rightly belongs. And as if that weren't enough—and it would be more than enough—"his divine power has granted to us all things that pertain to life and godliness" (2 Peter 1:3). What a generous Savior! Christ is the ultimate gift and the ultimate Giver!

Oh, that you and I would be captivated by Jesus. He is beautiful in every way. He is worthy of all that we are and have. He knows we will fail to worship him rightly, but—more amazing good news—he died for our lack of worship and apathy. The invitation remains open from him for us to come and receive, regardless of our unfaithfulness. He is always faithful.

The Cherished Bride

One cannot speak of enjoying Jesus without also thinking about the church. When people say "the church," there are a few things they could be speaking about, so let's define the terms. The Church universal is made up of those who put their faith in Jesus, people from all tribes and tongues and nations—and denominations! It is the community of all true believers for all time. God established the Church from the beginning (see Hebrews 11:4–32; 12:1). Jesus Christ builds the Church (see Matthew 16:18). The Church displays the glory and sacrifice of God—he sent his Son to die for the Church. The Church is made up of people who are united in Christ, brothers and sisters, adopted children of God. The Church will one day gather and sing praises to our King—together, united! It's glorious. And it is important.

Ultimately, the Church is important because Christ loves the Church and gave himself up for her (see Ephesians 5:25). We are the bride of Christ (see verses 31–32). What an incredibly beautiful picture of the love of Jesus and the importance of the Church. There are loads of metaphors for the Church in Scripture, but this one seems to capture the beauty and purity of the relationship between Christ and the Church. And one day he will present us as pure—like a virgin on her wedding day. Amazing!

The truth that we are the family of God is beautiful to write on paper and to think about. But when we look at how divided the universal Church is, it can be easy to become callous and jaded. Inside the Church there are theological debates and culture wars and confusion about various doctrines, and the list goes on. Some of the conflict and discussions are necessary and even healthy, but often it leaves me longing for heaven, where there will no longer be confusion and dissension. We will no longer see through a glass dimly. So until that day, we must learn to love our neighbor regardless of our differences.

Two of the biggest hindrances to enjoying the church that I've witnessed and experienced are conflict and time constraints. You and I are in church with fellow sinners. If you haven't experienced it firsthand, you've likely read about it. Pastors and leaders fall into sin, congregations divide over preferences or theological debates, abuse takes place, and so on. Beyond these big troubles are one-on-one conflicts that result in wounded people and ruptured relationships. As a pastor once said, relationships are a mess worth making.

Though church life can be challenging, it is still important, not only because of Jesus, but also because it is the means God uses to gather his people together and to further advance his kingdom. It is important because you and I together make up the body of Christ; each part is individually needed to advance the whole (see 1 Corinthians 12:12–27). In order for the Church to truly function, it needs you and me to be the feet, eyes, or mouth—the Church needs everyone functioning and contributing in some way.

The church is where we worship, take communion, and hear the spoken Word. It's where we minister to others through encouragement, love, comfort, and correction. The church is also a place where we can minister to unbelievers and share the gospel. One wonderful function of the church is to care for the orphan and widow and give to the needy.

Jesus gave his life for the Church. You and I have an opportunity to die to ourselves and in a sense give our lives to the Church through service to others. This service could look like laying down preferences, or it could be meeting with a sister who needs care.

Enjoying the Church through service may seem daunting, perhaps because in the past we've said yes to too many things. Programs, meetings, and service projects fill our calendars until we are depleted of energy and resentful of our pastors or even other members we think aren't pulling their weight. Part of enjoying the Church is asking God and others to help you discern where you might serve and then acknowledging your limitations to do it all.

God is a God of restoration. We will one day worship together as the Church universal. No more sin. No more confusion. No more division. Only unity and love. Worshiping together with a truly pure heart. No comparison, just Jesus at the center of our focus—forever.

The Gift of the Holy Spirit

As we wait for restoration to be complete, God has given us the Holy Spirit to help us discern where to serve, to help us worship in unity, and so much more. To enjoy God we must also learn to believe in and rely on the Holy Spirit.

The Spirit seems to be all too often left out of the equation when we think about God. We speak about God the Father, Jesus, and even God's Word, but it's rare that I hear a sermon about or read about his Spirit. As I've thought more about this, I've realized that without the Spirit we would be unable to enjoy God at all.

The Spirit has many functions in the Christian life. He is the comforter and helper (see John 14:26; 14:16), he teaches us (see John 14:26; 1 Corinthians 2:14), he grieves over sin (see Ephesians 4:30), and he interprets prayer (see Romans 8:26–27). But perhaps the most unique and impactful way the Spirit enables the Christian to enjoy God and all the aspects of God is that he dwells in our hearts (see 1 Corinthians 6:19; 2 Corinthians 1:22). We are no longer strangers, but instead we are daughters, and as daughters we have access to the Father through Jesus and have the ability to experience and enjoy all the benefits of this amazing union by and through the Spirit: "And because you are sons, God has sent the Spirit of his Son into our hearts, crying, 'Abba! Father!' So you are no longer a slave, but a son, and if a son, then an heir through God" (Galatians 4:6–7).

THE DISCIPLINES OF JOY

Though there are many ways we can delight in and enjoy God, I want to focus here on worship, prayer, and the Bible.

As we seek to delight in God, it's important to clarify that it's *not* about earning his approval or favor. This leads to the pitfall of legalism in our worship: pursuing good works with the intention of earning God's favor. For example, you read Scripture so that God will love you and be pleased with you and that your standing with him would be secure as a result.

When we work hard in order to earn God's favor, we are not operating with faith. Instead, we are saying that we must add to the finished work of Jesus on the cross. That his work wasn't enough, and therefore we must work to make him happy by, in this case, spending time delighting in his Word.

But the Bible says we are justified by grace through faith alone, and it is not a work of our own but a free gift of God. Our salvation is not, and never will be, a result of our works or how often we read our Bibles (see Ephesians 2:8). There is nothing we could ever do to earn God's saving favor. If we are in Christ, we have his favor, forever!

This may seem like a tangent, but the moment we begin addressing spiritual disciplines such as Bible reading and prayer, it seems the fear of legalism creeps up. Practicing the spiritual disciplines is one way to enjoy God. It is not legalistic *unless* it is motivated or driven by the thought that it can earn favor before the Lord.

You should certainly be aware of the temptation toward legalism as you practice spiritual disciplines. But remember that pursuing God should not be neglected, because our hearts are tempted to err and we need help to battle sin. How do we fight any temptation? We recall what God has done in Jesus and what he promises to do, which is all by his grace, not by our works. So you and I are free to read God's Word to learn about him, we are free to worship and pray, and we are free to enjoy him without concern that we are trying to earn salvation or favor.

Enjoying Worship

So often when we think of worship we go straight to song. Singing is an incredibly valuable and significant aspect of worship. The Psalms are filled with hymns to the Lord. I love hymns and enjoy playing them throughout the house as I cook dinner. When we miss any portion of our corporate worship service, I'm quite disappointed. Gathering with a body of believers to sing praises to our God is a highlight of my week. Yet worship shouldn't be relegated to just singing. Worship encompasses all of life.

Paul gave us a vision of worship beyond our voices:

> I appeal to you therefore, brothers, by the mercies of God,
> to present your bodies as a living sacrifice, holy and
> acceptable to God, which is your spiritual worship. Do not
> be conformed to this world, but be transformed by the

renewal of your mind, that by testing you may discern
what is the will of God, what is good and acceptable and
perfect. (Romans 12:1–2)

Our worship of God is about laying down our lives. This is not
a works-based worship. In other words, we can lay down our lives
only because of and by the mercy of God. So worship is knowing
and then acting on the knowledge that God is worthy of our admiration, our devotion, and our attention through our words and actions. He is worthy of our worship because of who he is.

There is joy to be found in surrendering ourselves to our Lord
through grace-fueled worship. There is freedom to enjoy all that
God has made us to be in him and to enjoy the benefits of God.
We can praise and sing with David,

Bless the LORD, O my soul,
    and all that is within me,
    bless his holy name!
Bless the LORD, O my soul,
    and forget not all his benefits,
who forgives all your iniquity,
    who heals all your diseases,
who redeems your life from the pit,
    who crowns you with steadfast love and mercy,
who satisfies you with good
    so that your youth is renewed like the eagle's.
        (Psalm 103:1–5)

What a good and awesome God! It is our joy and honor to
delight in the Lord. He pours himself out to us over and over

again. Forgiving, healing, redeeming, crowning—God is good!
His steadfast love endures forever. As you remember these things,
aren't you compelled to worship and enjoy him? And remember,
God is God. He owes us nothing. He is the Creator of the universe, holy and just, righteous and pure. He doesn't need us, but
he loves us. He didn't have to sacrifice his only Son, but he did.
What an awesome God we get to enjoy now and for eternity. And
because of Jesus we can draw near to the throne of grace and enjoy
God through prayer.

Taking Pleasure in Prayer

I've chatted with plenty of friends who are concerned about doing
the will of the Lord. Their concern isn't about a reluctance to obey
but about being sure to accurately discern what God's will is. This
is a common question and understandably so. We don't see everything God sees, and we don't know all that he knows, so we must
step out in faith. I'm so thankful for God's Word, however, as we
think about his will for our lives.

In 1 Thessalonians we read, "Rejoice always, pray without
ceasing, give thanks in all circumstances; for this is the will of
God in Christ Jesus for you" (5:16–18). We may not know what
job to take next or where to live or who to marry, but we do know
that God wants us to rejoice, give thanks, and pray without
ceasing.

Think about the access you and I have that we can pray without ceasing. God invites us to come to him day or night—anytime
we need to. I sometimes stumble in my words. I'm thankful that
in my weakness, when I don't know what exactly to say, the Lord
knows and the Spirit intercedes for me (see Romans 8:26). As I've
been teaching my kids to pray, one of the most common phrases

they say is "Mommy, I don't know how." In helping them understand how to pray, I could teach them the Lord's Prayer (and I will), but I've decided to start even more basic: I ask them simply to speak. I tell them they can talk to God.

To pray without ceasing isn't to present lofty words and eloquent speeches to God. It's to have a posture of prayerfulness and to recognize our need of him at all times. We can enjoy God simply by the sheer fact that we can come—wearily, joyfully, simply, however we are. What an amazing God we serve! What an incredible God we rejoice in!

Delighting in His Word

One of God's sweetest gifts, besides himself, his Son, and his Holy Spirit, is his Word. Scripture is God breathed. Both the Old and New Testaments are his words that reveal himself to us (see 2 Peter 1:21). The Scriptures are useful, binding, relevant, and true (see 2 Timothy 3:16–17). The law is perfect and revives the soul (see Psalm 19:7). The Lord uses his Word to bring people to himself (see Romans 10:17). God has been gracious to give you and me access to know many things about him: his creation, his desires for us, and, most important, his Son. Are we reading and treasuring this precious gift? I don't want to prescribe a Bible study format, but I want to ask you to examine whether you desire to read God's words.

I have had seasons of Spirit-filled, worshipful, and consistent times in the Word and seasons when reading has felt like a duty rather than a joy and delight. I've had seasons when I've gotten up at 5 a.m. to read, study, and pray. And I have had seasons when I was happy just to get in the shower and feed the kids.

I have some good news and maybe some bad news. The news

is this: we aren't necessarily after spiritual highs every time we engage God's Word. If you approach the Word with the mind-set that if you don't *feel* something, then you aren't *getting* anything from it, you won't read it. Once you change the focus from yourself to God, it's not only proper but it's also freeing.

We find joy in Scripture not because it makes us feel good but because it leads us to the One who spoke it into existence. Please don't misunderstand: there's nothing wrong with feelings. God created those too! I think it's good and fine to pray for a sense of awe and worship, but let's not rely on feelings to determine whether we've "gotten" anything out of our time with God in the Word. Most definitely, we must realize that our feelings do not determine our standing before God.

The Psalms open up with this declaration of true happiness: "Blessed is the man who walks not in the counsel of the wicked, nor stands in the way of sinners, nor sits in the seat of scoffers; but his delight is in the law of the LORD, and on his law he meditates day and night" (1:1–2). The man, or woman in our case, is happy to walk in the counsel of the Lord. Her delight is in the law of the Lord. She finds joy in it and is blessed by it.

To be clear, you and I don't deserve a blessing because we've delighted or obeyed. Grace is free, and God blesses whom he chooses. So we delight and are happy simply because we are already so very blessed by the Lord, who has poured out his mercy and grace. And how do we delight and enjoy the law? By meditating on it day and night. This doesn't mean you walk around with your Bible open every minute of the day. It means the Word is implanted in your heart and you are thinking and pondering his good ways as you go about your everyday life. Although this psalm is directed toward the Torah (the law), we can apply the wisdom in delighting in all of Scripture because, as we know, *all* Scripture is God breathed and profitable (see 2 Timothy 3:16).

The good news for you and me is that we have eternity to learn. We don't have to know all things right now. Actually, we can't know all things now; only God does. So don't be hindered by the fear that the Bible is too complicated for you. God isn't after lofty speech and great knowledge; he desires your heart. Run after him through his Word. The pressure is off! We have the joy of obedience and delight.

ENJOY THROUGH ABIDING IN CHRIST

I hear the phrase "abide in Christ" mentioned a lot by women as a way to express rest. At least, I *think* that's what they mean. The truth is, I've never had this phrase defined for me clearly, even though I've heard it shared so often. In order to gain more understanding, I started digging into God's Word to see exactly what it says about abiding in Christ.

Beginning in John 13, Jesus gave a series of farewell addresses that continue until chapter 17. He knew he would soon be lifeless on a tree, the crucified King. And in the middle of it all, he graciously reminded us that to be his means to bear fruit, and we bear fruit by abiding in him.

In John 15 Jesus described himself as the true vine, his Father as the vinedresser, and his followers as branches of the vine. The true vine was a way to contrast Jesus with Old Testament Israel. The original hearers of his message would have understood that Jesus was declaring himself to be *the* Messiah and the fulfillment of the covenant, because of the Old Testament references to a vineyard (see Isaiah 5:1–7; 27:2–6).

Jesus explained that the branches that do not bear fruit are taken away, but the branches that bear fruit are pruned to bear more fruit. To bear fruit simply means to grow in character—to become more like Christ and to reflect the fruit of the Spirit (see Galatians 5:22–23). And this is where we come to his command to abide: "Abide in me, and I in you. As the branch cannot bear fruit by itself, unless it abides in the vine, neither can you, unless you abide in me" (John 15:4).

Before Jesus got to the meaning of what it means to abide in him, he gave us a picture of what it looks like *not* to do so: "If anyone does not abide in me he is thrown away like a branch and withers; and the branches are gathered, thrown into the fire, and burned" (verse 6).

I guess I'm what you might call a plant killer. I purchase plants and try to care for them, but I often fail miserably. I forget to water the plant, depriving it of needed nourishment. And then one day I turn around and there it is, withered away. This didn't happen overnight. It happened after a season of neglect. One by one, the withered branches fall from the plant.

This, I think, is a picture of what Jesus was revealing in John 15:4–6. He explained that by not abiding in him we are like my pitiful plants: we will stop bearing fruit and soon wither entirely because we're not connected to the vine and so cannot get the nourishment that comes up through the roots of the vine. The fruit of the vine (or lack thereof) is proof of our faith. In this world we won't achieve perfection, but we should desire and pray for fruit, even if only a small bud. The fruit that Jesus speaks of is simply evidence of a relationship with him, a relationship that he initiates through and by his sovereign love.

In verse 10 we finally get a picture of what it looks like to abide in Jesus: "If you keep my commandments, you will abide in my love, just as I have kept my Father's commandments and abide in his love." So to abide in Jesus means to keep his commandments, and to keep his commandments means to love God with all our hearts and souls and minds and to love our neighbor as ourselves (see Matthew 22:37–39). One way we display our love for God is through our trust, prayer, and devotion to him. We abide through relationship. We pursue in love. We pray in love. We obey in love.

And here is the good news: We love Jesus because he first loved us (see 1 John 4:19). We didn't choose him; he chose us, and he chose us to walk out our faith in obedience to him (see John 15:16). Apart from Christ, we cannot do anything (see verse 5). This is also good news to the weary person who thinks she must muster up strength to pursue Christ and to love him. We are dependent on him to provide the grace and the strength.

In that same chapter, Jesus went on to remind us that there is no greater love than someone laying down his life for his friends. He then said, "You are my friends if you do what I command you" (John 15:14). Jesus tells us that we are his *friends* (let that sink in for a minute) if we obey his command to love, and that command is fulfilled through abiding. As we abide in him, we will bear the fruit of righteousness, the evidence of a transformed heart. And the offer to be a friend of Jesus—the Author and Perfecter of our faith, the Alpha and Omega, the Beautiful One, the One who bore our sins and transgression—is an irresistible invitation to enjoy him.

Abide in him, and he will abide in you. He who began a good work in you will complete it (see Philippians 1:6). "He who calls you is faithful; he will surely do it" (1 Thessalonians 5:24).

~

I'd like to ask you to stop before you move on to the next task, the next to-do on your list, even the next chapter in this book. Would you pause and ponder the beauty of our Lord? Think about who God is. Ask yourself why this God would be mindful of you and me. Rejoice in his goodness. Thank him for his faithfulness. Worship through song if you would like. Whatever you do, don't let another second go by without pondering the amazing goodness and grace of our Lord and Savior. When you do this, you'll discover just how much there is to enjoy about God. What a blessing that what we do in part today we will get to enjoy for eternity.

The Enjoy Project:
Delighting in the Giver

You will notice there are eight prompts this time instead of seven. This was intentional. There are so many aspects of our Father to explore and enjoy that I didn't want to leave any out!

1. Evaluate your current Bible reading habits. Is there anything that needs to be adjusted? Why is it good to read your Bible, and how can you pursue this while also resting in the grace of God?

2. Find a time each day this week to read your Bible, and schedule time one day to both read and study.

3. What aspects of the Church, universal and local, have you struggled with in the past or maybe even today? How have these struggles or troubles hindered your view and enjoyment of the Church?

4. Knowing that we are the body of Christ, made up of many parts, think of one way you might contribute to the life of your local church this week, such as encouraging, serving, or bringing a meal. Then do it.

5. What are some challenges you face in prayer? What have you gained from the discipline of prayer? Find a time each day this week to pray in a new way, such as writing down your

prayers or kneeling at the foot or on the side of your bed.

6. Meditate on who God is. See how many characteristics you can name and describe. Thank God the Father for who he is. Do the same for Jesus and the Holy Spirit.

7. Look back over the chapter to identify one idea or truth that really stands out. Find a way to put that into practice this week.

8. Taste and see that the Lord is good! Pray and preach the gospel to yourself.

How can I ever thank and praise you enough, Father, for who you are and what you've done? I don't love you because of the things you've blessed me with; I love you because you first loved me and sent your Son to rescue me from death. Throughout history, you've given. Help me to glorify you, to shine a spotlight on you with my life, just as Jesus did. Thank you for the freeing, beautiful truth of the gospel.

My *worship* **grows** and **grows** as my *perception* of God grows. God cannot grow.

My perception of God grows as I *experience* Him **day after day.**

—A. W. Tozer

Everlasting Enjoyment

*I*f I could sum up this entire book in one sentence I think it might be this: enjoyment is not about us; it's about God. You and I enjoy, not because we deserve good things or even because we have good things but because we recognize the grace and goodness shown to us by the Giver of all things. Our delight and joy in God is ultimately a reflection of God's delight and joy in what he has created. It is yet another way that we reflect God as his image bearers.

But how do we get from enjoyment for the sake of enjoyment to delighting because God is awesome and ultimately worthy of thanksgiving and praise? It may help to look at the Preacher in Ecclesiastes and his views on vanity and gifts, which we touched on briefly in the opening chapter.

The Preacher in Ecclesiastes seems quite conflicted. His words mirror our own wrestling with the now-but-not-yet reality of God's kingdom. Through Jesus's death and resurrection, God has begun the process of restoring the earth, but that process will not be complete until Jesus returns. We are already a part of his restored kingdom, and yet we continue to struggle through the realities of the Fall. We are already a part of the family of God, but we are not unified completely. We are already seen by our Lord as righteous, but we are not yet fully glorified and without sin. There's much for you and me to long for, and like the Preacher in Ecclesiastes, we could conclude that life is all just vanity—a vapor that will vanish and is meaningless.

The Preacher was not in need of anything. He was extremely wealthy. He fully indulged his flesh with work, food, drink, and experiences. He was also wise. And yet despite having every need met, he was deeply disappointed by life. You'll see a theme in reading Ecclesiastes: all is vanity of vanities (see 1:2) and "What does man gain by all the toil at which he toils under the sun?" (1:3). Even with his wisdom, the Preacher lamented that though it is better to be wise than foolish, the end for both is the same—we all die (see 2:12–16). Initially his thesis seems to be that everything will pass away, our toil is difficult, the world is evil, we may make no impact, we'll likely be forgotten, and so everything we do is vanity, pointless, and utterly worthless. But even with his recognition of the effects of the Fall on humanity and the world, he also repeatedly acknowledged that these things—work, food, play, wisdom—are gifts from the Lord, meant to be enjoyed (see 2:24–26; 3:22; 5:18–20; 9:9–10).

One statement from the Preacher stands out to me: "There is nothing better for a person than that he should eat and drink and find enjoyment in his toil. This also, I saw, is from the hand of God, for apart from him who can eat or who can have enjoyment?" (2:24–25). Yes, apart from God our toil would be worthless and enjoyment would serve only the flesh. He is the Giver of all good things and allows for our enjoyment of them. It is good and right to readjust our thinking and remember the good that

God has given to us—and not only remember it but also *enjoy* it as a means of worship.

The Preacher also acknowledged that God makes things beautiful in time (see 3:11). Life isn't going to be perfect here or even perfectly beautiful, but God is in the process of making all things new, and we have something to look forward to.

LOOKING AHEAD

When thinking of heaven, many of us swing between two extremes: We cling tightly to and seek pleasure in the things we can touch and see on earth, forgetting that we have a great inheritance awaiting us and doubting that anything could be better than the here and now. Or we constantly complain, discontent because nothing is perfectly good—ever.

Instead of swinging on this pendulum between pleasure seeking and misery, we can seek a balance between these two extremes. As we wait until that day when we see our Savior face to face, when the wrong of the Fall is corrected, when we will be glorified and no longer battle sin, we wait as those with hope. We have joy and peace because we know he is coming. We don't despair at the state of the fallen world we live in, but neither do we put our hope and faith in anything less than almighty God.

HOPE IN GOD

If you and I are to wait rightly for that day when our joy will truly be complete, we must hope in God. That means fighting the temptation to hope in ourselves or in our circumstances or in our possessions. Enjoying the good gifts that God gives us is not the same as hoping in them. None of God's good gifts will fulfill our every need, except for one: himself. Every other gift is icing on the cake. But none of them can or will satisfy us.

Recently, I got a tangible image of this reality. My son was thrilled to receive a Kindle for Christmas. We shared his excitement because we knew it would allow him to do more of what he already enjoyed doing—reading! Well, as it so often goes with technology, one of the features on his device didn't seem to work. Our posture quickly turned from excitement to frustration. Thankfully our son didn't despair as we scrambled to figure out how to fix it. He could have easily pitched a fit—it was a gift, and it wasn't doing what it was supposed to do—but that gift was never meant to satisfy my son. He wasn't placing his hope in this little device. As we've already explored, any idol, whether a small thing like a Kindle or a major life adjustment like a job change, can replace God and become our hope.

As you and I fight this temptation to treasure the things of earth above God, let's remember this key verse in Matthew:

> Do not lay up for yourselves treasures on earth, where
> moth and rust destroy and where thieves break in and
> steal, but lay up for yourselves treasures in heaven, where
> neither moth nor rust destroys and where thieves do not
> break in and steal. For where your treasure is, there your
> heart will be also. (6:19–21)

Your treasures in heaven will never malfunction. They will never rot and won't be destroyed or be able to destroy you. They will be perfect. Ask God to help you have a heart that treasures your future grace.

Maybe right now you aren't particularly tempted by temporary pleasures. Instead you might be thinking, *Everything in life and on this earth stinks.* Certainly we have reason to lament. As we've already considered, the whole earth is groaning. We should all be experiencing a sort of righteous discontent about the state of this world. This is not our home, and we should be longing for our next one. But as I noted earlier, we do not long and wait as people without hope.

We can rejoice in suffering because we have a living hope that will bring us to an eternal glory. We will one day rise and be with Christ *forever.* We can rejoice in suffering today because we know that "suffering produces endurance, and endurance produces character, and character produces hope, and hope does not put us to shame, because God's love has been poured into our hearts through the Holy Spirit who has been given to us" (Romans 5:3–5).

And this is the beauty of our hope: it is secure!

Who shall separate us from the love of Christ? Shall tribulation, or distress, or persecution, or famine, or nakedness, or danger, or sword? As it is written,

"For your sake we are being killed all the day long;
we are regarded as sheep to be slaughtered."

No, in all these things we are more than conquerors through him who loved us. For I am sure that neither death nor life, nor angels nor rulers, nor things present nor things to come, nor powers, nor height nor depth, nor anything else in all creation, will be able to separate us from the love of God in Christ Jesus our Lord. (Romans 8:35–39)

Nothing can separate us from the Lord. That's our awesome hope. We will be with him forever! So we endure suffering and loss and we adjust our view of any gain or gift because of the surpassing greatness of knowing Christ Jesus our Lord (see Philippians 3:7–8). He is our hope! He is our joy! He is our gift!

This is my prayer for you and for me: "May the God of hope fill you with all joy and peace in believing, so that by the power of the Holy Spirit you may abound in hope" (Romans 15:13).

HEAVEN BOUND

Death is such a mystery. We don't know what to expect, and we don't know when it will come. But we know that unless Jesus returns soon, we will experience it. Most of us, if we are honest, have a measure of fear when we think about the end. But as we dive into the Word of God and learn about this amazing place the Lord is preparing for us, we can't help but exclaim with Paul that to live is Christ but to die is gain (see Philippians 1:21). In death we gain Jesus.

The greatest joy in heaven will be seeing our Savior face to face. "Father, I desire that they also, whom you have given me, may be with me where I am, to see my glory that you have given me because you loved me before the foundation of the world" (John 17:24). What an incredible prayer from our Savior. He longs for us to be with him, and God delights to give us this gift. God has commanded us to love him with all our hearts and minds and souls, and there isn't a person on this earth who has ever obeyed this great commandment 100 percent. But this will not be so in heaven. When we see him, we'll love him, delight in him, and *enjoy* him perfectly forever. It will not be burdensome or twisted by sin.

Right now our earthly citizenship seems so sure and true. We can't go anywhere without some identification: We carry our driver's licenses with us at all times. We have Social Security numbers or something similar to identify us. We have addresses where we receive letters, or at least junk mail. But one day we will leave it all behind and head to our true citizenship in heaven (see Philippians 3:20–21). And this isn't any old place. Jesus said,

> Let not your hearts be troubled. Believe in God; believe also in me. In my Father's house are many rooms. If it were not so, would I have told you that I go to prepare a place for you? And if I go and prepare a place for you, I will come again and will take you to myself, that where I am you may be also. (John 14:1–3)

He is preparing a house with many rooms for you and for me. Abraham was looking forward to this paradise. "For he was looking forward to the city that has foundations, whose designer and builder is God" (Hebrews 11:10). Think of the beauty of our earth, designed and built by God so that even the Fall couldn't completely obstruct its beauty. So imagine what awaits us in the new heaven and new earth (see 2 Peter 3:13). God is making all things new and beautiful and pure. Jesus will welcome us to a place without trouble or decay. He is coming for his bride, and it will be a glorious celebration (see Revelation 21:1–2). What God has prepared for us in heaven is greater than our minds could ever imagine (see 1 Corinthians 2:9–10).

As we've explored already, one of the greatest barriers to our enjoyment on earth is that we continue to battle with sin. We groan, longing to be clothed with our heavenly dwelling where we'll be with our God, in his house forever, without sin (see 2 Corinthians 5:1–8). When you are in his house, you will no longer worry with that raggedy old sin. Can you imagine enjoying people perfectly? All the strife that you now have will be gone. You will worship your Lord along with every tribe and tongue and nation (see Revelation 5:9; 7:9–10; 19:1–5). No more division and hate. You will no longer struggle with impure motives; you will love fully.

Your food will taste like a bit of heaven—really! And you will no longer have to say good-bye. You will rest and work and enjoy without fear or regret all the things you have trouble enjoying now (see 7:15; 14:13).

All your sorrows will be wiped away. No more tears. No more death. All joy—all the time. "He will wipe away every tear from their eyes, and death shall be no more, neither shall there be mourning, nor crying, nor pain anymore, for the former things have passed away" (21:4). If you struggle to picture this glorious day because of current troubles, join me in opening up your imagination and dreaming about that day. As theologian J. I. Packer wrote, "Scripture teaches us to form our notion of the life of heaven by . . . enriching our imaginings of that happy future by adding in every conception of excellence and God-given enjoyment that we know."[1] Everything bad will go away, and whatever sweet goodness you've experienced will only multiply. The magnitude of the delights and joys are too vast to comprehend. You will long for nothing.

You and I are made for this future place. Enjoyment will no longer be a project that we hope to learn from but a reality that we'll live in eternally because this is what we are made for—to glorify God and enjoy him forever.

Author Randy Alcorn captured this truth so well:

Each of us is made for a person. And we're also made for a place. Jesus is the person. Heaven is the place. Jesus lives in Heaven and is getting a place ready for us there. So if we look forward to being with Jesus, that's the same as looking forward to Heaven. Why? Because that's where we'll be with him. So whenever we think about being with Jesus, we're thinking about Heaven. And whenever we think about Heaven, we should be thinking about Jesus.[2]

I sincerely hope you can delight today, knowing that one day you will have the privilege of delighting forever. God truly is the Giver of all good things. He doesn't withhold from you now, and he has treasures for you even in the end. Rejoice, enjoy, and delight in the One who is to be treasured forever.

Thank you, Lord! You are worthy of our praise and adoration!

The Enjoy Project Wrap-Up

It's time to wrap up the project. As I mentioned in the introduction, The Enjoy Project is meant to be a tool to help us enjoy all that God has done and is doing in our lives and in the lives of those around us. Ultimately, my prayer is that through the course of the project and this book you were able to find new and refreshed enjoyment in our Savior. I'd hate for us to come to the end of the book and simply move on. Instead, I encourage you to come back to this from time to time, when you are in the nitty-gritty of life and need a refresher course on how choosing to enjoy can lead you into deeper worship. There is no shortage of trials and difficulties in life, and my hope is that revisiting this wrap-up down the road will serve as a reminder of the good things God has for you in his Son.

1. Read or skim your journal from the beginning to the end. Write down or reflect on what stuck out to you. What have you forgotten about? Where do you still seem to lack enjoyment? Where do you see your enjoyment increasing?

2. As you've most likely noticed throughout the project, many areas of enjoyment affect others. In other words, if you aren't enjoying one area, you likely aren't seeing God's work in another. How might that apply to what you are still struggling to enjoy?

3. You and I can't force enjoyment. Of the chapters, which one did you find hardest to incorporate in your life, and why? What might you ask the Lord to do in your heart or circumstance to help you find enjoyment? (Remember, enjoyment could simply mean finding peace or contentment in your situation. It doesn't necessarily mean finding happiness in every single thing.)

4. Of the things you identified in question 1 that you forgot about or struggle to enjoy, pick one or two and seek to apply the action steps within the related Enjoy Projects.

5. Choose one or two of the places you identified in question 1 where you've seen an increase in your enjoyment, and find a way to apply the actionable suggestions for that chapter's project.

6. From each chapter, think of one thing you'd love to continue to grow in or revisit throughout the year.

7. Do or write out whatever it is you learned from this time of reflecting over the course of the project.

8. This is the culmination of what I hope was a refreshing and maybe challenging time of learning to enjoy the life God has given us while waiting for the life yet to come. Pray and preach the gospel to yourself.

Lord, I long to be with you. The evidence of sin's effect on the world and on me is so clear; don't let this cause me to despair. I know that you are the Victor, that because of Jesus, death and sin are no longer my masters. You are. And I long for the day that I will be with you, and sin and death will be no more. Keep my eyes on you and help me reflect your Son more.

For the

Present is the point

at which time *touches*

eternity.

—C. S. Lewis

A Note from Trillia

*P*erhaps you've come to the end of this book and realize you have not personally encountered this glorious God I speak of. In the end, we all must appear before the Lord to give an account (see Romans 14:12). My prayer for you and me is that we will be found to know Jesus. If you have not placed your faith and hope in him, I encourage you to repent, which means to turn from your sin today, and ask Jesus to be your Lord and Savior. Find a Christian friend who can help walk you through the gospel.

Discussion Questions

Chapter 1: An Invitation to Enjoy

1. Why do you think enjoyment is an important aspect of living out your faith as a Christian?
2. Is enjoyment of God's gifts in life something you've embraced well or struggled with at times? What's made it difficult?
3. How have you seen sin affect enjoyment in your life?
4. What do you learn about God and his giving nature from the creation account in Genesis 1?

Chapter 2: The Gift of One Another

1. How have relationships been a gift in your life?
2. How have you seen the results of the Fall affect your relationships?
3. Which of the "one anothers" listed in the chapter has been the most difficult for you to live out? Why?
4. Reflect on Christ's experiences with relationships while he was on earth. How do those relationships encourage and challenge you?

Chapter 3: The Joy of Intimacy

1. What messages come from our culture about sex? What lies are you tempted to believe?
2. Is your belief and understanding of sex based more on what God has said about it or on cultural values?
3. Why do you think God gave us the gift of sex?

4. How can we share and live out a biblical, God-honoring sexual ethic in our world today?

Chapter 4: Created to Work

1. Are you more tempted toward overworking or laziness with respect to work? Why do you think that is?
2. Do you view work more as a gift that happened before the Fall or a curse as a result of it?
3. How has your view of work been shaped?
4. What are specific ways you can glorify God with the work you're doing currently?

Chapter 5: The Freedom to Press Pause

1. In what ways have you struggled at times to enjoy rest?
2. Our culture celebrates the idea of self-sufficiency. How is self-sufficiency incompatible with the gospel and detrimental in our pursuit of enjoying rest?
3. How have you seen the value and purpose of rest and play in your life?
4. Jesus promises that through him we can have spiritual rest. How does that truth encourage and challenge you?

Chapter 6: Money, Possessions, and Joy

1. Many of us have a complicated relationship with money. How would you describe yours?
2. Why do you think the Bible speaks so much about money?
3. How have you experienced being blessed by others with the use of their money and possessions?

4. Reflect on God's generosity toward you. How does that encourage and challenge you in regard to money and possessions?

Chapter 7: Taste and See

1. What examples can you think of for how God used food to provide, bless, and encourage people in the Bible?

2. Food can be divisive. How have you seen or perhaps experienced this?

3. What has been your experience with fasting? How does this discipline focus us more on God?

4. Reflect on the incredible varieties of food we've been blessed with. Share your favorites and thank God for this gift.

Chapter 8: All Creation Speaks His Name

1. Read Romans 1:20. How does the created world clearly display God's attributes?

2. How are you reminded of the effects of the Fall when you consider the created world?

3. Is your tendency toward creation one of consumption or cultivation? Why is that?

4. What is God's posture toward his creation? How does that impact you?

Chapter 9: The Art of Life

1. How much of a priority do the arts play in your life? How have you come to this place?

2. We need to set wise boundaries when it comes to the arts. How have you done this, or how will you begin to guard your heart?

3. It's easy to turn the arts into idolatry. How have you seen this in the world or in your own life, and what are the effects?

4. How have you seen God glorified through the arts?

Chapter 10: Delighting in the Giver

1. Have you ever struggled to enjoy God? What led you to that point and, if you're in a different place now, what brought you out?

2. How can legalism creep in when we're seeking to enjoy God? What are the effects of legalism?

3. What can happen when we allow our emotions to determine whether we're truly enjoying God?

4. How has a better understanding of how to enjoy God's gifts given you a deeper enjoyment of God himself?

Chapter 11: Everlasting Enjoyment

1. Like the Preacher from Ecclesiastes, how have you struggled with feeling like life is vanity? How did God guide you through that?

2. How often do you think about our future home as Christians? Is heaven something you're excited about? Anxious? Fearful?

3. Reflect on the promise of Revelation 21:4. How does that truth affect life on earth?

4. How has recognizing God as the Giver of gifts for our enjoyment transformed your longings and desires?

Acknowledgments

This is the sweetest and hardest part of writing a book for me. There are too many people to thank and a great chance that I'll miss someone. I am blessed beyond belief by the number of friends, family, and ministry partners who supported, encouraged, cried with, edited, laughed with—and did I say cried with?—me during this process. Writing *Enjoy* was a gift to me this year, and I'm grateful to God, our dear Father, who has taught me so much about himself and living with a view of his goodness and the everlasting goodness we will experience one day.

This book would not have been possible without the excitement and eagerness of my dear editor, Laura Barker. *Enjoy,* in many ways, is the anthem of my life, and I'm grateful she and the wonderful folks at Multnomah took a chance on me. Thank you, Ginia Croker, for your enthusiasm as well. I'll look forward to cycling with you one day soon! Thank you to the entire team at Multnomah!

Thank you, Erik Wolgemuth! It's great to be able to call my agent a friend, and I'm so grateful for you and your family. Thank you for your continued work, assistance, support, editing, and creativity that make my work so much better. Thank you for your contribution specifically to the Enjoy Project prayers—they are beautiful. My whole family appreciates you! And thank you to the entire Wolgemuth & Associates team. Seriously, no flattery here, you are truly the best!

Thank you to Dan Darling and Phillip Bethancourt and the

entire ERLC team for your support and allowing me time to write *Enjoy*. Thank you, Jed Coppenger, my pastor and friend, for your prayers and kindness toward me, even when I was doubting and discouraged. Thank you, Mark Coppenger, for the plethora of books that I promise to give back to you! Thank you to my small group for your prayers each week. Thank you to Courtney Reissig, Tony Reinke, Amy Maples, and Melissa Kruger for allowing me to run ideas by you, for your prayers, and for your encouragement. Catherine Parks, you are amazing, my friend! Thank you for last-minute edits and for being such a dear and good friend to me during and beyond this process. And thank you to Leah Parks for assisting with the initial research for this project.

Thern, my dear husband, you are amazing in the way you lovingly serve, lead, and care for me and our two children. Thank you for making life so enjoyable. I could not write and serve in any capacity without your guidance and support. I'm a blessed woman, and I thank God for you. I pray we will be enjoying one another for many years to come!

Notes

Chapter 1: An Invitation to Enjoy

1. Jon Bloom, "When the Perfect Comes," Desiring God, December 28, 2012, www.desiringgod.org/articles /when-the-perfect-comes.
2. Zack Eswine, *Recovering Eden* (Phillipsburg, NJ: P&R Publishing, 2014), 102.
3. *The Westminster Shorter Catechism,* The Westminster Presbyterian, www.westminsterconfession.org/confessional -standards/the-westminster-shorter-catechism.php.
4. We see this in Genesis 1:3–4, 10, 12, 17–18, 21, and 25. After God created something, he looked and reflected and said it was good. And then, the culmination of all he created resulted in *"it was very good"* (verse 31, emphasis mine).
5. Jeremiah Burroughs, *The Rare Jewel of Christian Contentment* (Carlisle, PA: The Banner of Truth Trust, 1964), 1.

Chapter 2: The Gift of One Another

1. "And now you are cursed from the ground, which has opened its mouth to receive your brother's blood from your hand. When you work the ground, it shall no longer yield to you its strength. You shall be a fugitive and a wanderer on the earth" (Genesis 4:11–12).
2. C. S. Lewis, *The Weight of Glory* (Grand Rapids, MI: Zondervan, 2001), 46.

Chapter 3: The Joy of Intimacy

1. Ed Wheat and Gaye Wheat, *Intended for Pleasure* (Grand Rapids, MI: Revell, 1997), 15.
2. Ellen Dykas, *Sex and the Single Girl* (Greensboro, NC: New Growth, 2012), 8.
3. Dykas, *Sex and the Single Girl,* 23.
4. Nancy DeMoss Wolgemuth, in a phone interview with the author, January 26, 2016.
5. As written by a friend specifically for authorized use in this work.
6. Leda Marritz, "How Deep Do Tree Roots Really Grow?" Ask Jim Urban, August 8, 2012, www.deeproot.com/blog /blog-entries/how-deep-do-tree-roots-really-grow.
7. Lou Priolo, *Bitterness: The Root That Pollutes* (Phillipsburg, NJ: P&R Publishing, 1995), 9–11.

Chapter 4: Created to Work

1. Timothy Keller and Katherine Leary Alsdorf, *Every Good Endeavor* (New York: Riverhead Books, 2012), 35.
2. Keller, *Every Good Endeavor,* 51.
3. John Piper, *Risk Is Right* (Wheaton, IL: Crossway, 2013), 15.
4. Sebastian Traeger and Greg Gilbert, *The Gospel at Work* (Grand Rapids, MI: Zondervan, 2014), 51.
5. Traeger and Gilbert, *The Gospel at Work,* 36.

Chapter 5: The Freedom to Press Pause

1. Tim Keller, "The Power of Deep Rest," The Gospel Coalition, November 25, 2012, www.thegospelcoalition.org /article/the-power-of-deep-rest.

2. Chris Isidore and Tami Luhby, "Turns out Americans work really hard . . . but some want to work harder," CNN Money, July 9, 2015, http://money.cnn.com/2015/07/09 /news/economy/americans-work-bush/.

3. Dean Schabner, "Americans Work More Than Anyone," ABC News, May 1, 2015, http://abcnews.go.com/US /story?id=93364&page=1.

4. Erik Thoennes, "Why We Play," The Gospel Coalition, September 26, 2014, www.thegospelcoalition.org/article /why-we-play.

5. Thoennes, "Why We Play."

6. Thoennes, "Why We Play."

Chapter 6: Money, Possessions, and Joy

1. Randy Alcorn, *The Treasure Principle* (Colorado Springs: Multnomah, 2001), 9.

2. Alcorn, *The Treasure Principle*, 75.

Chapter 7: Taste and See

1. Wayne Grudem, ed., *ESV Study Bible* (Wheaton, IL: Crossway, 2008), 2179.

2. Derek Rishmawy, "Delicate Tastes," The Gospel Coalition, May 16, 2014, www.thegospelcoalition.org/article /delicate-tastes.

3. Jonathan Edwards, "The Pleasantness of Religion," in *Sermons and Discourses: 1723–1729,* ed. Kenneth P. Minkema, Jonathan Edwards Center, http://edwards.yale. edu/archive?path=aHR0cDovL2Vkd2FyZHMueWFsZS5l ZHUvY2dpLWJpbi9uZXdwaGIsby9nZXRvYmplY3QucGw/Yy4xMzo2OjEud2plbw==

4. Edwards, "The Pleasantness of Religion."

5. Becky Wilson is the owner of http://sassyfeast.com.

6. Martyn Lloyd-Jones, quoted in John Piper, *A Hunger for God* (Wheaton, IL: Crossway, 1997), 16, 200.

7. Erik Raymond, "What Is the Purpose of Your Dinner Table?" The Gospel Coalition, October 26, 2010, www .thegospelcoalition.org/blogs/erikraymond/2010/10/26 /what-is-the-purpose-of-your-dinner-table/.

Chapter 8: All Creation Speaks His Name

1. Stephen J. Nichols, "More than Metaphors: Jonathan Edwards and the Beauty of Nature," *SBJT* 14.4 (2010): 48, 53, www.sbts.edu/wp-content/uploads/sites/5/2011/02 /sbjt-v14-n4_nichols.pdf.

2. T. M. Moore, "Every Square Inch," *Christian Worldview Journal,* December 12, 2012, www.colsoncenter.org /the-center/columns/talking-points/18933-every -square-inch.

3. Wayne Grudem, ed., *ESV Study Bible* (Wheaton, IL: Crossway, 2008), 2158.

4. Nichols, "More than Metaphors," 51.

5. Jacque Wilson, "Worst U.S. cities for spring allergies," CNN, March 31, 2014, www.cnn.com/2014/03/31/health /worst-allergy-cities-spring/index.html.

6. Nichols, "More than Metaphors," 55–56.

Chapter 9: The Art of Life

1. Francis A. Schaeffer, *Art and the Bible* (Downers Grove, IL: InterVarsity, 1973), 18.

Chapter 10: Delighting in the Giver

1. *The Westminster Shorter Catechism,* The Westminster Presbyterian, www.westminsterconfession.org/confessional-standards/the-westminster-shorter-catechism.php.
2. Michael Reeves, *Rejoicing in Christ* (Downers Grove, IL: InterVarsity, 2015), 9.
3. Reeves, *Rejoicing in Christ,* 10.

Chapter 11: Everlasting Enjoyment

1. J. I. Packer, *Concise Theology: A Guide to Historic Christian Beliefs* (Carol Stream, IL: Tyndale, 2001), 265.
2. Randy Alcorn, *Heaven* (Carol Stream, IL: Tyndale, 2004), 4.